John Vestal Hadley, John Hadley

Seven Months a Prisoner

John Vestal Hadley, John Hadley

Seven Months a Prisoner

ISBN/EAN: 9783744759717

Printed in Europe, USA, Canada, Australia, Japan

Cover: Foto ©ninafisch / pixelio.de

More available books at **www.hansebooks.com**

SEVEN MONTHS A PRISONER;

OR,

THIRTY-SIX DAYS IN THE WOODS.

GIVING THE PERSONAL EXPERIENCE OF PRISON LIFE IN GORDONS-
VILLE, LYNCHBURG, DANVILLE, MACON, SAVANNAH, CHAR-
LESTON, AND COLUMBIA, TOGETHER WITH A DESCRIP-
TION OF HOW NEW CAPTURES ARE RECEIVED INTO
PRISON, OF HOW THEY ACT AND WHAT THEY
DO, ETC., ETC., AND TWO ESCAPES, THE
LAST SUCCESSFUL, FROM COLUMBIA
TO KNOXVILLE, OVER
A DISTANCE OF

FOUR HUNDRED MILES,

EXTENDING THROUGH THIRTY-SIX DAYS, AND FRAUGHT WITH
MANY THRILLING ADVENTURES AND HAIR-
BREADTH ESCAPES.

CONTAINING NONE BUT ENTIRELY NEW ITEMS.

BY AN INDIANA SOLDIER.

INDIANAPOLIS:
J. M. & F. J. MEIKEL & CO., PRINTERS.
1868.

PREFACE.

In presenting this little volume to the public, the author claims for it nothing in a literary point of view. It has not been prepared for the library or the critic's desk, nor has it grown out of any desire for literary fame; but it is the legitimate offspring of the "embarrassing leisure" generally attendant upon the beginning of a profession. Its publication, however, is not so much to find employment, as to preserve in some kind of order for the satisfaction of ourself and friends, the adventures, hardships, and sufferings endured in an escape from Columbia, S. C., to Knoxville, occupying thirty-six days. This, then, being our principal object, we have thought proper to sketch very briefly, in a simple manner, but a few of the leading features of seven months confinement in rebel prisons, and if in our endeavors to tell the truth, we have exaggerated or obscured any material fact, to that extent have we fallen short of our aim. In some things mentioned we may not corroborate other writers upon the subject, for we have written in a spirit of liberality towards the jailors of the South, and with no other guide than a few imperfect notes, hence whatever discrepancies may appear, may no doubt be accounted for in the fact that we have labored, especially to evade a too vivid recollection of our treatment, to the end that we might deal impartial justice to our enemies, as well as to the generous and loyal hearts that aided us in our final accomplishment. So much has already been written upon "the treatment of prisoners of war," that we feel considerable hesitaation in adding anything more, and our silence in many matters we desire to be construed into a desire to save the reader from wearisome repitition. To detail all the crimes and barbarian cruelties that came under our personal observation, in the various prisons;

would take more time and more pages than we have leisure to write, or the public patience to read. To present something new, to prepare for the fickleness of old age, to enliven a sympathy for the loyalists of the South, and give recreation in an idle hour, more especially to the children, is the hope of

THE AUTHOR.

DANVILLE, IND., 1868.

CONTENTS.

CHAPTER I.

Jack Pendleton vs. Henderson—Grant's Last Campaign—The First Day's March—General Rice and his Staff—The First Guns of the Wilderness—Mistake of the Second Brigade—Lieutenant Mitchell—The Captured Mississippian—The Fury of Battle—The Climax.............. 1

CHAPTER II.

Parker's Store—Lieutenant Shelton—First Escape—Shelton's Strategy—The Wilderness Battlefield and its Dead—The Whip-po-wills of the Rapidan—The Grievous Mistake—Shelton Gives Out—Takes Refuge at Mrs. B.'s—Charley, the Rebel—The Ignominious Betrayal—Off for the South—The Thieves at the Rapidan—Shelton's Trouble with his New Clothes—The North Carolina Lieutenant—Shelton's Resolute Pluck—General Wadsworth—Shelton Left Behind—All Alone Now—Tim. Hayden—General Lee's Head-Quarters—Colonel Richardson—Yank—The Poor Indian—Gordonsville and Starvation—Charlotsville—Lynchburg—Pandemonium—Relic of the Institution—Danville—Jamestown—Bill Reese—Augusta—Macon—Camp Oglethorpe—How they Took us In—Who we Met Inside—The German Captain—Tunneling—The Fourth of July.... 14

CONTENTS.

CHAPTER IV.

Lieutenant Chisman—Off from Macon—General Stoneman's Raid—At Savannah—The Curious Populace — Drayton Street—Chisman and the Rebel Girl—The Prison—Major Hill and His Guard—How They Treated Us—From Savannah to Charleston—The 13th of September—Charleston Jail Yard—The Bombardment—Under Fire of Our Own Guns—The Desolation of the City—Yellow Fever in Our Camp—Consternation of Our Guards—Sent to Columbia—Intense Suffering from Thirst—The Rebel Refugees—The Cadets— Camp Sorghum — Amusements — Rations — An Officer Torn to Pieces by Dogs—The Final Escape...... 59

CHAPTER V.

Lieutenants Good and Baker—The Home Stretch—The First Night's Difficulties—Our Organization—The First Negro —Our First Interview—Chisman's Speech to the Darkies —The Saluda River—Quandary as to Route—Our Second Interview with the Negroes—Our Decision—Streets of Laurensville—The Irishman's Short Comings—Good and the Gander—Locked Up in a Barn—In Terrorem—Martin and Moses—Sumptuous Supper—The Two Cavalrymen—North Carolina Line— Fight Among Ourselves — The Hounds at Ross'—Reuben—Captain Pace and His Company After Us—Reuben's Fidelity—Collision with Captain Pace—Saluda Gap—The Guard in the Road—Flat Rock —Interview with Rebel Soldiers — How We Escaped Them—On a Lost Mountain, Lost, Starving and Freezing —The Culmination of Sufferings and Trouble—God Works in a Mysterious Way—The Union Girls—The Garret—Juan's Strategy.. 71

CHAPTER VI.

The Women of North Carolina—Waiting for Guides—The Candy Pulling—The Old Gossip—More Female Strategy —Adieus— Among the Robbers—Their Murders—Their

Cave—Their Engagement with Us—Why They had to Tarry—The Expedition to Dr.....—The Capture of One of the Vances—Our Hurried Departure— Crossing the French Broad River—Good and His Pone—Banks Burton's—His Neighbors and Family—Among the Mountains —The Obstinacy of Our Guides—The Majesty of Mount Piscah—Abandoned by Our Guides in the Wild Mountains. 132

CHAPTER VII.

South Hominy Creek, Buncombe County, N. C.—Uncle Jimmy Smith—That Day's Fight Between the Unionists and Rebels—George Peoples—Kim. Davis—Our Next Guide—Week in Buncombe County—Girls of Buncombe— Farewells in the Davis Family—Again in the Mountains— Sandy Mush—Rocky Ridge— Mr. Dunn—The Mules— Federal Pickets—Knoxville—The Old Flag—How We Felt—How We Looked—Gay Street—General Carter— In a Federal Hospital—Hood Besieging Nashville—Organization for Home, via Cumberland Gap—Kim. Home Again—Conclusion............................. 160

SEVEN MONTHS A PRISONER;

OR,

THIRTY-SIX DAYS IN THE GAUNTLET.

CHAPTER I.

JACK PENDLETON VS. HENDERSON—GRANT'S LAST CAMPAIGN—
THE FIRST DAY'S MARCH—GENERAL RICE AND HIS STAFF—
THE FIRST GUNS OF THE WILDERNESS—MISTAKE OF THE
SECOND BRIGADE—LIEUTENANT MITCHELL—THE CAPTURED
MISSISSIPPIAN—THE FURY OF THE BATTLE—THE CLIMAX.

Those who were with the 1st Division, 1st Army Corps, at Culpepper, Virginia, in the winter of 1863 and '64, will all remember Jack Pendelton, with his dogs, his parrots, and his race horses. Jack, without doubt, belonged to the F. F. V's. He not only said so, but his pedigree, which he often recited in our company, ran back through a collateral family of the Washingtons. He was 67 years old, his hair was white and silken, and hung down in massive clusters near a pair of broad, square shoulders, surmounting a body of comely proportions. He had been raised by, and lived always among slaves, with a whip or club in his hand, and his habit of command had grown into second nature in his dotage; and it was his egotistical and dictatorial address that makes him so well remembered by those soldiers who came under his notice. Jack was rich before the War; had many broad acres about Culpepper, and counted his slaves by scores. But, unhappily, he lay in the war path of the Potomac, and the armies, both Northern and Southern, marched and counter-marched over him for two years, so that at the time of which we write, perhaps not one rail could be found on his one thousand arable acres, and scarcely a dozen wagon loads of knotty pine and oak wood. His valuable negroes had ran away, their houses were torn down, his fine orchard destroyed, his garden and park laid waste, and a mile south of the Court House, upon a beautiful elevation, nestled among forest trees, in the midst of a vast desolated plain stood his sightly residence, which had still been spared. This house no doubt had been a seat of hospitality: for the long tables, the many broken decanters and the numerous horse racks at the gate, spoke it louder than the oft' repeated words of the host. Jack was an anti-secessionist at the start, but, probably, more from policy than principle, for in an able and eloquent speech, delivered in Richmond in the winter of 1860, his principal argument was the inevitable desolation of Virginia in the event of a war. He, too, had been a politician; had represented the Whig party of his District for two terms in Congress and had filled a foreign appointment under Taylor. He was the great personal friend of Abraham Lincoln; they had served in Congress together, and Mr. Lincoln, with a dozen other members, once went home and spent the holidays with him. This was the event that supplied Mr. Pendleton with many anecdotes, which he could tell in capital style. A half mile west of the house was the course where he beat Mr. Lincoln in a horse race; and twelve miles to the east was the Wilderness, which now contains more dead mèn's bones than deer, is the place where the party chased a deer for two consecutive days—Mr. Lincoln proving himself the noblest Nimrod of them all.

Four rooms in Jack's house—two below and two above, were now occupied by General Rice as Headquarters, and the writer of this sketch was doing duty on his staff. Our party, eight in all, upon the main, got along agreeably with the host, after our reconciliation; but when we first occupied, without permission, the old man suggested, rather emphatically, too, that he regarded it a summary proceeding, saying, "that when General Longstreet made his headquarters there but a few weeks before, he had the politeness to negotiate with him."

Jack was a rebel now, and most vehemently hated run away negroes. We had four or five of these at headquarters, who were constantly giving the old man trouble. Among them was a great big muscular African named Henderson, who had ran away from an old friend near Fredricksburg. Jack's hate especially rested upon this boy, for no other reason than he had left him whom he knew to be a good master. Henderson was a taciturn, obedient, inoffensive boy, and went about the premises doing errands, saying nothing to anybody, and had several times run when pursued by Jack. But he was finally forbidden the yard, and informed that if he entered it again, it would be upon peril of his life, and for several days went trudging around through the mud, while the other servants could pass and repass through the yard at pleasure. This forbearance ceased to be a virtue with Henderson, and he asked the General one day what he had done, or who he was that this distinction should prevail among them. The General, always on the side of the oppressed, told him to go about his business, and through the yard whenever his duty required it; that he must be polite and kind to the old man, but if Jack showed him any violence, to defend himself. This counsel was oil upon troubled water, and Henderson went from the General walking an inch taller than ever before, for it was the first time in all his life that he had license to fight a white man.

It was not more than an hour until there was a collision. Henderson had but time to get to our kitchen and black a few pairs of rusty boots, when he boldly started through the yard to deliver them. Jack, ever on the alert, met him, raised his cane, and, as usual, with a terrible oath, went to the attack, but this time to find battle instead of chase. Henderson parried, thrust, and down went the blooded Virginian to the ground, crying murder, and bellowing like a gored ox. Every body about headquarters ran out immediately, and what we saw was more ludicerous than serious.

We found Henderson sitting astride the old aristocrat, with knees upon his arms, and a lion's grasp upon his throat, counseling or shutting off his breath, as the case required.

The parties were summoned to trial—Rice sitting in judgment—witnesses sworn, white and black, in anticipation of the Civil Rights bill. The case was regularly tried, which resulted in the General giving an elaborate opinion adverse to Jack. This threw the old lawyer into hysterics; he raved, he swore, and he cried. Commanded the General to leave the house, or burn it with him in it; that he would rather perish in his own house than to be so insulted in it. Because Rice would not do either, Jack appealed to Corps Headquarters, but General Newton was always too much engaged to investigate it.

Jack went to Washington and Baltimore that winter. Notwithstanding his rebel proclivities his relations with Mr. Lincoln were sufficient to secure him the necessary pass over the signature of the President. His business was, ostensibly, to get family supplies. The morning he was to leave home he came into the dining room while we were at breakfast, with his high hat and scissor-tailed coat on, and remarked:

"Rice, I should expect a pleasant time with my friends

if it were not for that G—d Stanton ; he hates me, and if he finds I'm up there, he is almost sure to arrest me."

"Oh no," says R., "he would not think of it when he finds out that you are up there on invitation of the President."

He was to be gone two weeks, but three had well nigh passed before he returned. Mrs. Pendleton, an excellent and amiable lady, was much distressed at his absence, and to her great relief, one afternoon, Captain Lacock's wagon drove up and left at the door an eight gallon demijohn of whisky, two barrels of crackers, two or three of flour, one of hams, etc. Soon the old man was seen coming slowly over the hill, evidently out of humor. He passed in through the back door, and was not seen any more that day.

The next morning, while we were at breakfast he came in with his brow knitted and wearing the expression of a desperate man.

The General accosted him. "Why! good morning Mr. Pendleton. I'm glad to see you back. You staid longer than you expected to, did you not?"

"Yes. May G—d— that Stanton ; he arrested me, sure enough."

Some how Stanton found out that Jack was in the city and arrested him on the way to the cars, returning home, and detained him in prison a day or two, and until the President ordered his release.

On the night of the 23d of May, 1864, we broke the happiest camp ever occupied by the army of the Potomac. Man and officer felt as he drew off the little piece of shelter-tent which had formed the roof of his log hut, "well, we've had many a happy time in these quarters, anyhow.' And we had, too. We had had excellent rations, good clothing, and furloughs, three things as necessary to the good feeling of an army as discipline and victory is to its efficiency. Every one, too, seemed to appreciate the magnitude of the work before us.

Grant had been made General of the Armies, and coming from the West, flushed with victory, and flattered in his hold on policy, had established himself with us. He had concentrated large forces of foot and horse men, and to this end had made all the forts and bomb-proofs about Washington and Baltimore disgorge. These extraordinary preparations, together with a very suggestive order from General Meade, beginning: "Soldiers! you are again called upon to meet the enemy;" was conclusive enough to the dullest man that aggression was the plan of the campaign, and that when the Army of the Potomac moved, with its new leader, its power was to be felt and feared. The Army had perfect confidence in Grant, and in themselves. Although perhaps not so many victories were inscribed upon their banners, they never doubted but that they could fight as long and as well as the Western Armies, if led by the same genius. Nor for once did we believe, that when the much hated Rapidan was again crossed, that we would have to return as we had done twice before.

The order for our march was not unexpected, and found but few unready, yet it was not without some trouble that we made ready to move out—certain transfers of property to make, tents to turn in, pack mules to saddle, provisions to pack up, etc. But when midnight came we were all ready to fling our brigade into line. Our orders took us to Germania Ford, and in that direction the 1st A. C., now the 5th, was soon wending its way through and over the hills.

The night march was made without interruption, and next morning we made our coffee at Stevensburg, but eight miles from the Ford.

The morning opened up very warm. The road was dry

and dusty, and as the sun's rays fell scorchingly upon backs burdened with prodigious knapsacks, there fell in, on either side of the road, innumerable blankets and overcoats. Had some enterprising Quartermaster followed in the wake of this Potomac Army for two days he might have collected enough of such articles to supply at least one half the corps the coming winter.

About noon we crossed the Rapidan without opposition, and just on the other side halted in a pine grove to rest and cook some coffee. An hour was there spent, when we again moved out on the plank road leading to Fredricksburg. The march this afternoon was as labored as any I ever saw. The men, with the usual large loads carried on the opening of a campaign, and having had a long rest, made it very difficult for them to trudge along through the intense heat and dust. Many were overcome and fell by the way side, and many more were discouraged and sullen, so that before we reached our bivouac at Wilderness Tavern, the straggling was alarming. Our staff was ordered out to drive all stragglers to the ranks, and for one, I have spent few afternoons when my duties were more fatiguing. It was one continuous command of "move on!" and forcing up with the sword or revolver worn out soldiers, whose very countenance depicted extreme suffering. But at 5 P. M. the head of the column reached the Tavern, and after another hour's ride we succeeded in getting the Brigade in camp, and the roll called to the satisfaction of the Generals. We then rode off with General Rice to a little eminence capped with a cluster of pine bushes, and here picketed our horses and pitched our tents for the night. We were all dirty and tired, but after taking a good wash and putting on clean collars, we sat together upon a grassy mound, feeling happy, for our day's work had been satisfactorily done. But, for some reason, the General's usual humor and vivacity was wanting, and he seemed serious and downcast.

Lamdin said to him, "General, what's the matter? Are you unwell?"

"Oh, no! I'm just tired; that's all."

After drinking our coffee he said to us:

"Boys, all of you fill your pipes and come with me again to those bushes. I want to have a talk with you."

Rice was one of the few christian Generals. His Bible and evening prayer were no more neglected than his sleep. Though sometimes complained of for his petulence, he was, for the most part, a meek, kind, exemplary christian. Six of us sat down with him. He first asked each what his purposes and objects in life were after the war, and then proceeded in a lengthy, but excellent moral lecture. He exorted us to temperance and morality. "But beyond all, study honesty and integrity, which are the moving elements to sure success."

We carried with us two tents, one for the use of the General and his nephew, Lieutenent Bush, and the other for the rest of the staff, and we had them both pitched on this occasion, but after finishing our talk the General said:

"Bugler, sound Taps, now. Boys, let us all go into my tent and sleep together to-night, for it may be the last opportunity we will ever have."

By this time the spell had seized all of us, and we followed into that tent like those following a bier. We spread our blankets in one continuous bed, the General's in the center; and having seated ourselves upon them, the General read the ciii. Psalm, after which, having prayed fervently for our protection in the coming events, we laid down and went to sleep. Never did seven hearts seem to reciprocate more fully each other's interests; and never did better feeling bind "heart to heart and mind to mind."

There is an enchanting something in the soldier's life out of which grows more brotherly love, more pure unadulterated friendship, than can be felt anywhere else. Whether it springs from a common interest, or common aim, or whether from the probability of a sudden "taking off," or what, it certainly prunes the disposition and weeds the heart of all selfishness and jealousy.

A "still small voice" seemed to say to the General that on the morrow night five of the seven would be missing, and that in a few days he should be gathered to his fathers.

The morning of the 5th of May opened up very fair. A few guns reported early three or four miles to the southward, where General Crawford lay with his division. Rumors were current that Lee was falling back to Gordonsville, and the firing was supposed to be on his rear guard. But events that followed soon proved that this supposition was wrong. At an early hour we moved out in the road, in the direction of Crawford, but had not gone more than two miles before we met an aide hurrying from Crawford with the news that the enemy were advancing through the Wilderness, close upon us. Our regiments were at once double-quicked into line, batteries thrown into position, wagons sent to the rear; and in five minutes everything presented the appearance of work.

In the meantime the general directed me to cover the brigade with skirmishers, wich I did by taking five companies of the 95th New York, and two companies of the 76th New York, and deploying them four or five hundred yards in the front.

We were now fairly in the ill omened Wilderness. So dense was the foliage, that the skirmish line was entirely obscured from the line of battle. Matters went on until 11 o'clock A. M., without any appearance of the enemy, and General Warren, commanding corps, somewhat doubt-ting the correctness of the report, rode up and said :

"General Rice, you will advance your brigade skirmishers two miles south-west, and if you find the enemy before reaching that distance, hold all the ground you gain until the line of battle gets up; you moving your line forward as soon as the firing begins."

Similar orders had been given to all the brigades of our division: and General Rice turning to me said:

"Lieutenant, you will see that these orders are executed?"

I replied by calling for my horse: but at the same time looking significantly at my friend Chisman, who was lying at ease on the ground. He well knew that I had been in the saddle my full share that morning, and well read in my looks, my wishes, for he sprang to his feet with:

"General, with your permission I will assist Lieutenant ——— in advancing the skirmishers."

"I would be very glad if you would, sir," was the answer, and he joined me before I reached the line.

We moved off in conjunction with the skirmishers of the 1st brigade on our right, carefully feeling our way through the woods. We crept along for a mile as noiselessly as possible, making or hearing no sound louder than the cracking of a bush, when suddenly an owl in our front went "hoot, hoot, hoot." "Hallow," says Chisman to me, "that owl is not used to his song, or he could do better than that." "Hoot, hoot, hoot," went another, away off to the right, and we hurried along the line and told the boys to keep a sharp lookout. A few rods further on, and the next signal was, bang, whiz, spat, from a rebel musket. The enemy was at hand; and whether we fired the first guns on that great campaign, is no matter, but right here began the bloody battle of the Wilderness.

A brisk firing at once began in our front, and soon it extending along the whole line. The results were various

—charging and being charged, advancing and retireing; two or three times our line was broken like a reed, and hurled back several hundred yards; and it was in trying to withstand one of these violent onsets, that my horse received a shot in the hip, which made him almost unmanageable. For fifteen minutes we had it hot, and yet no sign of the brigade coming up. We had no protection on our left, and the rebels overlapped us on that flank, we knew not how far. For a slight protection we swung back fifty men, at right angles with the front, yet, with this, a thousand men might have marched around to our rear, and swept off the last man. A volley of musketry broke forth to our right, probably in the rear of the 1st brigade. Roar after roar came rumbling through the forest, shaking our hearts with fear, for a thought came into our minds that it might be our bigrade that had mistaken the direction, or the whole line had borne too much to the right, and left us without support. At this time Lieutenant Mitchell rode up from the General and confirmed our fears, for he said that he had left the brigade but a few minutes before, away to our right, within a short distance of the skirmishers. He also bore orders from the General to hold out if possible. While Mitchell was with us, the rebels charged us again, and were repulsed, as we thought at the time, along the whole line of the brigade, but subsequent events proved that they had succeeded in driving back a hundred men of the 1st brigade, immediately on our right, the density of the forest preventing us from discovering the fact. We begged Mitchell to make haste to represent to the General the exposed condition of our left flank, which not only endangered us, but the whole army. He dashed away to return again in five minutes, with the Generals orders thereon. We waited in painful suspense five minutes, and he had not come—ten minutes, and there were no signs of him; dangers thickening about us the while. I called to Chisman that I would go myself and see what was the matter, and what we should do.

I galloped off to the right, in the direction of the battle, as fast as I could, dodging under the limbs and from the trees, and had not gone far, when about crossing a beaten path I chanced to glance to the left, and there stood a man within thirty feet of me, in the path facing the rear, with a musket hanging in his right hand. Not noticing him very closely, it occurred to me in the moment that he was a skulker from our skirmish line, and I yelled out at him, "What are you doing back here, sir?" Whereupon he replied:

"Are you a Yankee, sir?"

A rebel—quick as thought I jerked my horse to the left, plunged both spurs into his sides, snatched my revolver, and in a twinkle was upon him. He jerked his musket to his shoulder, but in his hurry had failed to raise the hammer, and before he could recover and raise it, he had to jump out of the path to keep from being ridden down, and before he could rally I had my revolver pointing at his breast, with a demand for his surrender. His gun fell to his side, and I then commanded him to double quick to the rear. All possible haste was made to get him away from there, for I feared that he might have comrades close at hand, who would come to the rescue. Having hurried him to the rear a few hundred yards I began thus to interrogate him:

"What were you doing out there, sir?"

"My duty, sir."

"Who placed you there?"

"My officer."

"Were you alone?"

"Perhaps not, sir?"

"What regiment do you belong to?"

"Eighth Mississippi."

He was a soldier who knew well his duty—not to give the enemy information. He turned back to me at one time, with a most malicious look, and said:

"Well, I'll be d—d if you are making much off of me."

"Why," said I.

"Because, sir, I had the exquisite pleasure a few moments ago of escorting one of your officers to my Colonel!"

"What kind of a looking man was he?"

"He had on fine clothes, had a moustache, a red badge on his breast, and was riding a roan horse."

Mitchell's delay was now accounted for—poor fellow, he had reported to the wrong man.

I first found a regiment of the Pennsylvania Reserve, thrown out as flankers on the left of the line of battle. Here I left my prisoner, and dashed up in the rear of the first regiment engaged, which proved to be the 147th New York, one of our brigade. The battle was raging in its fury. Colonel Miller had just fallen, and the Major but a few minutes before, and had been carried back. It was only after a dozen efforts that I learned from a Lieutenant that the General had just gone up the line. Bullets were hissing and hitting everywhere. My horse was wild as a ranger. I headed him northward, gave him the rein; for the sooner he took me out of there the better he would please me. He went flying through the timber, squatting and dodging at the bullets and trees. While in full speed, a ball struck him near my leg—saw him fall—saw his nose plough along the ground and double under his breast—I saw or remember no more.

CHAPTER II.

PARKER'S STORE—LIEUTENANT SHELTON—FIRST ESCAPE—SHELTON'S STRATEGY—THE WILDERNESS BATTLEFIELD AND ITS DEAD—THE WHIPPO-WILS OF THE RAPIDAN—THE GRIEVOUS MISTAKE—SHELTON GIVES OUT—TAKES REFUGE AT MRS. B.'S—CHARLEY, THE REBEL—THE IGNOMINIOUS BETRAYAL.

Boardman, of the 147th New York, told how it was: "In the rear of their regiment my horse was killed while in full speed, and, in falling, threw me against a tree, then pitched headlong against me. Soon after my misfortune our battle line gave way, and the enemy possessed the place and me."

We will next begin at Parker's Store. This place is now in history; not from its importance, but for the events it witnessed.

An old house, built fifty years ago, sits by the thoroughfare leading down from Fredericksburg to Orange Court House, in the midst of a cleared spot of five or six acres. All around it is the wilderness. If Mr. Parker was a merchant, and had customers, it is a novel question where they came from; for truly, I do not believe there were a dozen families in a dozen miles' radius. Business had been suspended and the place deserted many years, no doubt, for much of the roof had fallen off, and here and there a weatherboard was swinging by one end. This was Parker's Store, where, on the 6th of May, 1864, lay one thousand rebel and fifty Federal soldiers, bleeding and dying.

I awoke, as if from sleep, about 7 o'clock in the morning. I tried, but failed to get up. My left eye was entirely closed, and I had a misery in my left breast and shoulder. I was hurt, but knew not how or how much. The first thing that attracted my attention was a column of troops hurrying along the road silently, but on a forced march. What! have they gray clothes on? No; it is my injured sight. I rubbed my eyes and tried it again, with the same result; then I turned on my elbow and looked around me. Those immediately near had on the blue, as had also a soldier bending over a prostrate form with a canteen.

"Soldier, come here. Am I a prisoner?"

" Yes."

I asked no more questions, but lay back, and was a little more willing to " give up the ghost," just then, than I ever expect to be again. I had no hope; mortally wounded, no doubt, and in the hands of the enemy, to be tortured unto death; or, if I recovered, they would send me south, in the hottest months, to some prison pen, to starve or die of epidemic. But I was not so badly injured as I had at first thought. My head and left breast were badly bruised, but it was the excessive loss of blood that made me feel so near the end. Had I been in a Federal hospital I would have been up in twenty-four hours; but mush and gruel, and a very small piece of bacon, were three days in getting me on my feet, and for five days more I went moping about, though mending faster than I appeared to be. It was a rule of the hospital, as fast as the prisoners got able, to send them south. As strength returned to my body a notion came into my head to escape. I wanted to be free. My idea was, that it would be more easily accomplished from that hospital than anywhere else. I did not make much ado about my convalescence; in fact, I said nothing about it, and nobody else was concerned.

On the morning of the 13th the doctor made his rounds for those to be sent south. For some reason, best known to myself, I was still quite bad; but my feebleness was more on account of prison pens and short rations than injuries. He felt my pulse, looked at my tongue, sounded my breast, shook his head, and went off.

Fifteen minutes afterward I was lying by Lieutenant Shelton, of Battery D, 1st New York Light Artillery, arranging for our escape. He was wounded in the leg, below the knee, but ambitious as a Bonaparte. He was young, and had been but recently promoted, and the love of honor with his battery was stronger than the fear of rebels, or of losing his leg by an eighty miles tramp to Alexandria.

Said he: "If you are going to-night, I am going with you."

He was the ablest one in the hospital, but, much as I desired company, I seriously doubted his ability for the task. But we arranged to go at dark. During the day, Shelton traded a jack-knife for a pone of corn bread; Colonel Miller gave us a compass, and Lieutenant Hamilton a map of Virginia. I say gave—for we had nothing to give in exchange. My sword, my revolver, cap, knife, pocketbook, handkerchief, diary, even my tooth brush were all gone as booty to my captors.

When night came, we took adieus and messages from our suffering comrades, and went off the back way into the woods. There were but few guards to give us trouble; here and there went a patrol about the camp or hospital, and there was a picket post a few hundred rods off on each direction of the road. We learned enough during the day to elude all the posts, and had caution enough to follow close after one patrol and be gone before another came along. We slipped noislessly through the woods until we had passed the picket post, then we went on the road and headed for Alexandria. We much desired to keep the woods altogether, but the brush and bushes constantly hurting Shelton's leg, we found it impracticable. Shelton locked his arm in mine for support, and with a stick in the other hand seemed to get along with but little difficulty.

About a mile on the way we came to another field hospital by the road side, and seeing nobody astir, we continued straight on; but while the lights from the hospital fires were still shining on our backs, suddenly there came ringing from the front:

"Halt!" and a guard stood in the middle of the road before us.

"Let's go back to the hospital; my leg is hurting me," said Shelton loudly. And we turned about and went back without further disturbance. Having cleared the hospital again, we entered the woods, slipped around the fires, and returned to the road—this time, beyond the picket.

The road led us across the battlefield, and the noisome smells announced it long before it was reached. We would have shunned it had there been any chance—but there was none. The rebels had told us of its condition, and like every one that had lost friends there we shuddered at the thought of seeing it. The stench—it was awful—that is enough to say. Men and horses lay thick in the road in process of natural decay.

"Right up there, on that mound, is where I lost two guns and my liberty," said Shelton; I must go up to the spot again."

We went up, and there lay men and horses thicker than ever.

"This body is Corporal Tole; he fell at my very side. This one is George Mullen, No. 2 at the gun. This other is Sergeant Linden. He veteranized and married but a month before. Now, let us step down to those bushes and see the last of cousin Henry Stiles; the dear boy was killed dead while carrying me off the field."

The body was half submerged, but we lifted it tenderly out to a dryer spot to crumble. Shelton then examined every pocket for some relic for the broken-hearted mother, but the theiving enemy had been there before, and none could be found.

We lingered in the society of the dead for an hour, and verily it was a task to leave them. Like the dog on the plains, that finds society and will starve by his dead master's side. For, as ghastly as these decaying bodies appeared in the moonlight, there were spirits that seemed to arise from them to hold communion with us. They were all strangers to me at this point, but had I known where the bones of Thomas Ashby, of John Doyal, of William Reynolds, of John Hornaday, of Henry Hoadly, of Captain Clayton, and many other friends were resting I should have been constrained to see them before leaving the field.

We decided to cross the Rapidan at Ely's Ford, and from Wilderness Tavern we took the road to that point. Our strength, stimulated by excitement and hope, lasted us wonderfully. The further we went, and the faster we went, the smarter Shelton seemed to get. We had no other disturbance during the night, and at 3 o'clock a. m. we sat down to rest upon the bluff, one hundred yards from the Ford, having traveled nearly twelve miles. Our object was to reconnoiter the Ford by daylight, before crossing, lest there be a picket on one side or the other. Oh! that horrible May morning. With all the serious impressiveness of the battlefield we had just passed upon our minds; sick and sore; within the enemy's lines, and probably within a hundred yards of his muskets: in the stillness of the night; by this ill-omened river—these things made us cling together like two lost children, starting at every sound. Then there were those birds, in countless numbers, whose songs are said to be melodious, but which seemed to us, on that night, like the cries of so many devils, sweeping up and down that dismal river, screaming without ceasing their "whippo-wil, whippo-wil, whippo-wil."

As soon as it was light enough to distinguish an object on the other side, we pulled off our boots and crawled down to the Ford. We listened for several minutes, and no sign or sound of human being coming from the other side, we arose and stepped into the water. But we did not listen quite long enough; most unfortunately, we started across five minutes too soon; for before we got to the other side, a man came running to the south bank, shouting at the top of his voice:

"Halt, there! halt!! halt!!!"

How happy we would have been to know that this man was a member of Captain Bryant's company, of the 5th New York Cavalry, whose company being out on a scout, had stopped upon the hill to breakfast and feed, and this man was coming to watch at the Ford for the time. The thought never entered our minds that he could be anything else but a rebel, and we ran for dear life, not even taking time to put on our boots; but over the hill we flew, and into the wood, entirely forgetting our debility.

Heretofore I had been a support to Shelton; now, I shouted to him to wait. We continued to run for more than a mile, fearing they would pursue us, and took refuge in the midst of a pond between two hills. It was a favorable place to hide, being covered with a dense thicket, yet the spot where we rested was elevated and dry, but proved to be in unpleasant proximity to a house, for soon we heard the murmuring of voices and hallooing of children upon the opposite hill. We feared they were rebels hunting for us, and we lay down upon our faces as still and noiseless as two logs. My exertion in the morning had re-opened the wound in my breast, and I had a frightful hemorrhage in the bushes. Shelton's leg, too, began to swell and pain him. That which seemed as hideous to us this day as the song of the whippo-wil, was the never ending, never varying croaking and chattering of the frogs. They hopped about us, and over us, and one ugly creature had the impudence to perch himself upon my friend's back and tune his harp.

Two or three times snakes glided along, shaking their tongues in our very faces, and yet we felt that we dare not stir to destroy them. A dog, too, chasing a rabit, ran upon us, but, to his credit, turned away without barking. All day long we heard the noise upon the hill, and all day long we lay quiet. A cloud came up in the afternoon, and poured torrents of rain down upon us for two hours. It saturated us from head to foot. The water raised over our little island, but we took seats upon a log and held out until nightfall. Shelton's leg had swollen terribly, and was feverish and painful; but after the rain he kept it submerged, which afforded some relief.

When dark came we crawled out of the bushes and briars, and after a little rambling found and took the road leading to Kelly's Ford of the Rappahanock. The night was cloudy and dark, and the roads slippery and rough, but the increasing hope of escape gave us strength to get along briskly. Twice we met horsemen in the road, but by stepping into the bushes eluded them. Once we met some citizens in a wagon; they had been "picking up" in the Federal camps, and were talking loud about their victory at Spottsylvania, and the killing of General Sedgwick. Our aim for the night was to cross the Rappahannock at Kelly's, and reach Mrs. M——'s, where we had previously made our headquarters, and where I believed we would find some favor—a thirteen miles journey.

Several times I asked Shelton how he was getting along.

"Oh, first rate," he always replied, and a time or two refused to rest when I was anxious. But about midnight he began to hang heavier on my arm. I asked nothing about it, thought nothing about it; for he had so often assured me that he was doing well, I had no doubt of it. The hope of soon being over the Rappahannock, among trusty friends, and in a country little infested with rebels, so completely occupied my mind that I could not think of the possibility of a calamity near at hand. Yet it came, before the morning, from a source I little dreamed of.

"H——, my leg is killing me. I must sit down," said Shelton about 2 o'clock in the morning.

We had traveled distance enough to have reached Kelley's, but had taken the wrong road at the forks, and were now three miles away.

Shelton's leg was fearfully swollen; so much so that it was impossible to raise his pants without splitting them. After resting some time we tried it again, but Shelton now found it more difficult and painful to walk than when he stopped. It was next to impossible to go at all now, and in persisting in it he could see inevitable loss of life or limb. He gave up in despair, imploring me not to forsake him in that helpless condition. The weather was quite cold, and our clothes being yet wet, we decided to build a fire and remain by it till morning.

When daylight arrived we discovered a house within a

few hundred yards, and after a little reconnoitering found it to be the house of Mrs. B——, of good Union report. A column of smoke was already ascending from the chimney, and a lady was chopping wood in the yard. We concluded that I should assist my friend to the house, ask for concealment, and if granted, I should stay with him until able to go on; if denied I should leave him and proceed alone. With my aid, and that of a stick, we succeeded in reaching the house. We were met by Mrs. B—— and five children, three of whom were young ladies. The war had impoverished, but not dispossessed the family of goodness. They received us kindly and sympathetically, and readily accepted our proposition for concealment.

"Yes; I could not think of turning you away, lest my iniquity should sometime be visited upon my dear Charles, who was driven into the rebel army."

We were shown into the house, to seats before an old fashioned Virginia fire place. Every hand was set to work in doing something for us. First, hot water and bandages. Second, clean, dry clothing. [I may mention here that the house was within sight of the camp lately left by one of our corps, and from whence Mrs. B——'s family had collected large supplies of abandoned clothing and meat.] Third, some army coffee and "hard tack."

Soon Shelton's wound was dressed, both had on dry suits, and a satisfaction of breakfast, and then we might have been seen crawling up into an old ricketty garret to hide. A comfortable bed was spread for us up there, and we were directed to feel perfectly secure, as the entire family would observe the strictest secrecy in the matter. The old lady, particularly, was most profuse in her attentions to both. The wound was bathed and poulticed a number of times every day, and the greatest care observed to provide such food as was best suited to our condition. Our own mothers would scarcely have done more. Seven days did we lay in that garret, a profound secret, only in the family, and in a few days more would have renewed our journey.

In the meantime Charles, the son, a member of the 5th Virginia Cavalry, had been at home twice, and hardly a day passed but what more or less rebels had eaten dinner below. They belonged to Stuart's command; and I add to the shame of our arms, had been sent into Culpepper county to pick up deserters from our army. The number of these cowards that ran away from the battle in the Wilderness was alarming. They had to take refuge in our old camps to get something to eat, and one day, through the little window in the garret, we counted twelve of them in one gang. One party of five called at Mrs. B——'s inquiring for rebel soldiers—they wanted to surrender. Another squad of three came in one day, with their guns, and demanded dinner or blood. I must say, however, that these scoundrels were mercenary substitutes from eastern regiments, who had no more desire for the honor or the success of the Federal than the Confederate arms.

Although Charles had been home twice since our concealment, he had not the slightest inkling of the matter. A third time he came about 2 o'clock in the afternoon, having ridden his horse, as he averred, twelve hours without a feed. He remembered some corn which his mother had hidden in the garret for bread, and, without consulting her, made for the ladder. His mother caught him before he got up, drew him back, and was obliged to tell him all. She elaborated the circumstances; who we were, what we had done for her, and what the rebels would do for her in the event that they should find out that she was harboring Yankees. They would burn her house, drive them from the country, and perhaps lodge them all in prison. Charles fully understood it all, and assured her that he should observe the strictest secrecy. The good old woman was perfectly delighted, was very sorry she had so long kept her secret, and brought Charles up and introduced him as an "additional friend, her son, from the rebel army."

As proud of Charles as his mother seemed to be, I did not like his manner, and Shelton liked it less. He was "as mild a mannered man as ever scuttled ship or cut a throat," young, and had some "gift of gab." His conversation was as plaintive as a minister in his first year, and he really seemed more distressed about our condition than we were ourselves. He remained with us an hour sympathizing, moaned when he saw the hole in Shelton's leg, and sighed when I coughed. In taking his leave he was *so* hopeful that we would give ourselves no concern about our safety; that we should stay content until able to go; that we would reach our lines in safety, etc. And chief among his kindnesses he also insisted that we remain at least a week longer, when he would be back home again, that he might take his horse, a mighty trusty fellow, and set us over the Rappahannock some night. He over did the matter. When he spoke to his sister below, Shelton turned to me and said:

"——, if you think you are able to cross the river tonight, I will consent that you leave me, for that fellow will betray us."

The mother soon returned to the garret to reassure us of Charley's fidelity—he was always a good boy; that she would stand between us and danger from him, etc.

It can hardly be believed when I add that the villain was back in less than an hour, with three other rebel soldiers and two extra horses, to carry us to some hospital on the other side of the Rapidan, and would have done it immediately had not the good old lady interceded for us. She was a mother who loved her son, but seemed just then to love honor more. The treachery of the scoundrel appeared as much to the distress of his mother as to us. She cried, she talked, and she abused the wretch handsomely.

"I want you to go back to your regiment, and stay there, and never come home again, if it be only to abuse the confidence of your mother."

A compromise was effected by the intercession of the old lady, wherein it was agreed, upon the part of the rebels, that we should remain there a week or ten days, or as much longer as was necessary to improve our condition sufficiently to be moved without danger to life or limb; and on our part, to give our paroles of honor " not to leave that house until ordered to by a Confederate officer."

The paroles were written and signed, and there was some distribution of Shelton's effects; one thief started away with his boots, but the old lady intercepted and recovered them.

There was nothing but trouble at Mrs. B——'s the balance of that day. The mother and sisters thought they could never forgive Charley; and then there was fear that the rebels would visit some punishment upon them for harboring us. The good woman avowed that before the week was out, she would have some conveyance to carry us to the other side of the Rappahannock, and send us on to Alexandria; that we should not be so mercilessly betrayed in her house.

But it was not in the Divine arrangement of things that we should then succeed in escaping. The second day afterward three others came with orders from some Colonel on the other side of the Rapidan to bring us over, dead or alive. There was no alternative now. There was no compromising with this party. Mrs. B—— thought there was, for she repeatedly asserted that we should not go. She knew not what arbitrary things military orders are, and because the guards persisted in taking us at once she called them "heartless dogs."

We did not go, however, until that magnanimous good woman had supplied each with two shirts, two pairs of socks, towel, soap, blanket, and myself a cap. With these things before us, on the horse, she approached us with streaming eyes, and we took her hand, perhaps for the last time.

I have never heard of Mrs. B—— since that time, and probably never will again; but I have this tribute to write of her: She was loyal in Virginia, a Christian in works, and a faithful friend in adversity.

CHAPTER III.

)FF FOR THE SOUTH—THE THIEVES AT THE RAPIDAN—SHELTON'S TROUBLE WITH HIS NEW CLOTHES—THE NORTH CAROLINA LIEUTENANT—SHELTON'S RESOLUTE PLUCK—GENERAL WADSWORTH—SHELTON LEFT BEHIND—ALL ALONE NOW—TIM. HAYDEN—GENERAL LEE'S HEADQUARTERS—COLONEL RICHARDSON—YANK—THE POOR INDIAN—GORDONSVILLE AND STARVATION—CHARLOTTSVILLE—LYNCHBURG—PANDEMONIUM—RELIC OF THE INSTITUTION—DANVILLE—JAMESTOWN—BILL. REES—AUGUSTA—MACON—CAMP OGLETHORPE—HOW THEY TOOK US IN—WHO MET INSIDE—THE GERMAN CAPTAIN—TUNNELING—THE FOURTH OF JULY.

It was back across the Rapidan and towards Lee's Army, which had by this time crawled back near North Anna, we were taken. We were received at Germania Ford by a guard from the other side, who met us midway the stream and demanded our boots. One fellow threatened to drown us if we did not pull them off before passing the river, and a second gathered Shelton by the foot, and cried to his comrade:

"Dave! hold that hoss while I pull the boots off this d—d Yankee."

But Dave wanted the boots too badly himself to co-operate and so the river was passed without the much coveted treasure being secured by any one. I do not blame them much for wanting Shelton's boots, for they were new, and an excellent pair, fine, high, and beautifully stitched, such as even Yankee soldiers would delight in pulling from the feet of rebels, and just such as every newly fledged lieutenant buys. Poor boy. He had scarcely worn his boots and straps a fortnight before his capture, and to lose his first official clothes before they had lost their lustre, was deplorable. He did not lose his boots here; but he lost what was worse--his straps and jacket. The Lieutenant in command, a North Carolinian, (and I am sorry I have forgotten the name) did not need the boots himself, and protected them; but the lustrous jacket suited him well for the summer's campaigh, and with all complacency he stepped up with—

"Yank, pull off that 'ar coat. I want to try it on."

Earnest remonstrances proved fruitless, for the rogue would have nothing but the jacket. So, off it came, and in its stead on went a long-tailed, coarse, brown, jeans coat, which Shelton had on his back when he ran the gauntlet of the rebel guard line, at Columbia, six months afterwards.

I fared much better at the hands of these rebels than my comrade, for the old, weather-beaten garments I had on were unenviable, and I had but little trouble. This was the out-post of the rebel vidette, and they were in communication with Lee's army, forty miles off—the posts standing five miles apart. Here we lost our horses, and had to take it afoot to the next post. I managed to get along pretty well, but poor Shelton suffered terribly. His wound had been suppurating most profusely for four or five days, and was swollen to twice its natural size; yet, if he murmured once, or asked one favor from the mounted guards, I have forgotten it now.

We were reported to the next post, a written receipt asked and given for two Yankees, and in fifteen minutes more, we were on the next five mile stretch. By this time I was very much fatigued, and my injuries were hurting me some; and had I not felt that it was "go and live, or stay and die," I certainly would have had some rest. But on we went, without a halt, and I was as much spurred on by Shelton's pluck as rebel sabres.

The task, however, was too much. This brave boy dragged along while there was strength enough in his poor body to move, but at last sank down in the road and gave it up. The heartless wretches that had us in charge, tried to drive him up with their sabres, and one villian, drawing his revolver, cocked it, and held it directly at his breast with—

"—— ——, you, move on, or I'll blow your heart out."

The heroic courage of this boy here, was worthy of a martyr; for as great as the impending danger seemed to be, as much as he suffered in body and mind, asked no respite, uttered not one complaint, nor asked any assistance or favor at the hands of his enemies. After some parley, one of the guards dismounted, put Shelton on the horse, and soon we were again under way.

Before reaching the third post we were taken across a part of the field of the Wilderness that had been fought twenty days before. It was a dense forest on either side of the road—not a man or beast had been buried by either army, out of that vast number killed—and, not enough that death should strike them low, but a devouring and relentless fire had swept over the field, burning the hair and garments from the dead, and the hope of life from the wounded; and now that three weeks had passed, and the worms done their work, a thousand skeletons, in black, charred shrouds, with empty eye sockets and glaring teeth, seemed to mock us, and cry out, "we were murdered in the flames." If there is one cruelty that I suffered at the hands of the rebels that I cannot forgive, it was the wanton act of driving us over that battle-field, with no other object than to add one more thorn to our already suffering condition. But we got through, and the next time we halted was at post No. 3, a rebel field hospital, a few miles south of the Wilderness battle field. Here we were lodged for the night, and shown where the old hero and patriot, General Wadsworth, paid the price of his patriotism. Here, in this solitary, nameless spot, in the midst of an ill-omened forest, without a pillow or a tear, on the 7th day of May, 1864, died an old man who had given more to his country of fortune and life, than any man who had ever lived in it. The artificial parts of this hospital was such as may be found in the midst of most forests; near a little murky brook, with no shelter but the branches of the trees, and no bedding but leaves. There were about four hundred wounded men grouped together here, and among them twenty Federals, all badly wounded. Shelton's leg by this time was painful in the extreme, and I was suffering what I would have considered among my friends at home, nearly death, but here I was able to go to the brook for a canteen of water and dress my friend's wound. In the meantime, a negro in attendance had prepared us some mush, and after having eaten a liberal quantity, (for it was the first of anything we had had since leaving Mrs. B's.) we stretched ourselves together near an old log, feeling the cords of friendship bind us closer and closer, as we expected to be parted in the morning.

That memorable night was full of horror to me; expecting next morning to be driven further South, alone and a prisoner, weak and suffering, and without even the presence of a Federal soldier to encourage me. This seemed enough; but to add tenfold, my sleep was either broken in that frightful lonesome place, by the moans or demoniac yells of the suffering wounded, or the curses of the annoyed guard, or disturbed by alternate dreams of home and cruel jailors and horrible prison pens; and as much as I hated to see the dawn appear in the east, to separate me from my friend, I could not wish it delayed.

That night, wakeful as we were, some rogue got Shelton's cap, and before he left there they also got his boots, so that when we met again, six weeks afterwards at Macon, Georgia, his embroidered cap was supplanted by an old greasy wool hat, his new jacket by the veritable brown jeans; his boots by a pair of sun-burned, sun-cracked, rusty brogans of the Southern army style.

Sure enough, next morning Shelton was unable to move; so, when I had taken my allowance of mush, I pressed his hand "farewell" and resumed my march to Dixie. As feeble as I was, they got me over eighteen miles before sundown, to post No. 7, where I was receipted for by a Virginia Captain, a rather clever fellow, who, at my request, kept me over night. I was very weak and tired when I sat down upon the grass with the Captain; but after having drank a cup of his hot coffee and eaten a piece of soft bread and cold ham, and taken a "few drops" of Virginia hospitality, I felt invigorated and talked an hour about the war. At eight o'clock I wrapped my blanket around me and slept soundly the entire night.

The next day I expected to reach Lee's headquarters, and I much wondered how I should feel, or what I should see in that *invincible* Army of Northern Virginia, that had been talked of so much since my capture. I was off again at 7 A. M.; was feeling better than the day previous, and got along with more ease; my guard was kind, and let me rest frequently. About noon we reached post 8, just after the relief had returned from picket. I do not know the emergency to dispatch me in such a hurry; but the officer in charge seemed determined that I should proceed at once the remaining four miles, to the headquarters of the Army. The men had just fed their horses and were setting themselves about for dinner when the officer, probably out of fear for his own haversack, called to one of his men to saddle his horse and report me to Col. Richardson. This the man did not feel inclined to do until after dinner, and he was not very polite in expressing himself. He swore he would not, and his officer swore he should. The soldier's horse had not been fed since yesterday, and he himself had had nothing warm to eat since supper, besides he had done more duty than the rest that day, and was unwell. The officer did not agree with him, and a perfect war of oaths was waged for ten minutes before the horse was saddled.

To assist me in the good graces of the soldier, I remarked to the officer, that I was very tired, and should like mighty well to rest half an hour, while the guard cooked his dinner. But it did no good. His dignity rested upon his autority, and *go now* he had commanded, and *go* we should.

Sluggishly and sullenly the guard crawled into his saddle, persisting that he would not take me far, and muttered to a companion near by.

"I 'low to kill the d—d Yankee as soon as we get to the woods."

"Rack out, here!" were his words—and I racked. "Faster," and I quickened a little; all the time trying to appear as if I regarded his threats as mere jests, while, in reality, I was in the most perfect terror. This incident makes me smile now, but when it occurred there was anything but humor in it. Few know how I felt. The prisoner led to the place of execution, and pardoned on the spot knows; and perhaps no other, for when I thought how angry he was, and how he might shoot me in the woods, under pretense of my trying to escape, I had not whereon to hang a hope. My mind was as active as it was distressed. I thought of nearly everything in a minute, and decided that if I would escape his vengence, I must flatter him into favor.

On I went, in a dromedary pace, he cursing me every step.

"My friend, I am a very poor walker, and very much out of fix, and I do wish you would give your horse and me a little more time," "the war won't be over to-day," I remarked.

"Hurry on, sir—I intend to give you all the time you want, when I get you into the woods," he replied.

This opened my heart afresh; but, bracing myself up again, I continued:

"Oh, I would rather have my marching a little more distributed—I stand it better, and can make more distance in the end;" and further added: "that officer of yours must be a heartless dog to treat you as he did back there. If an officer in our army were to abuse and curse one of his men as that fellow did you, he would be at work on the Dry Tortugas in less than a month."

"Yes," said he, "he is a—rascal!—a young pimp who drove a few niggers around before the war, and now thinks he must drive soldiers around the same way—the first time we get into a fight I bet I'll stop his fun."

"From what I had heard of you rebs, I supposed you were all such men as he—cruel and cowardly to a prisoner, but, verily, he is the only one I have met since my capture who has not treated me like a gentleman."

"What regiment do you belong to?"

"Second Virginia."

"Ah, I have heard of your regiment before. You fought our cavalry at Kelly's Ford. I have heard our dragoons say that yours was the only regiment of Southern cavalry they feared, and moreover, when one of our wounded soldiers was captured at Kelly's, and some North Carolinians had robbed him, a party of the 2d Virginia came up and made them restore everything they had taken, and since then your regiment has been held in high esteem in our brigade."

Thus the conversation went on, and I could soon see that I was getting a hold on him. Nearly three years in the army had taught me that to gain a soldier's esteem and awaken his pride, was to incidentally speak of the gallantry of his command; or if you wish to awaken his wrath to violence, speak of its cowardice.

I made a perfect conquest, as the gentle reader will perceive when I add that before we had gone two miles of our journey, or before we had passed that much dreaded woods, I was mounted upon the horse, and the guard walking at my side.

Tim. Harden was by all odds the roughest mannered rebel I ever had directly to do with; but in him was a faithful exemplification of the old maxim: "the harder the hull, the sweeter the kernel." When I reached his heart I found it full of kind offices.

We found Colonel Richardson about 3 o'clock, p. m., snugly at rest in a marquee, with half a dozen well dressed rebel officers about him. I was led into their midst, receipted for as one Yankee, and the guard dismissed.

Colonel R. raising his spectacles and pen, asked:

"What is your name and rank, sir?"

"* * * My rank is First Lieutenant."

"To what command did you belong, sir?"

"To the staff of General Rice?"

"Indeed! It occurs to me that we have already here a relic of General Rice's headquarters. Bob, go and bring Yank. here."

Now, I was in a quandary—a relic of General Rice's headquarters, and an order to "go bring Yank. here." Was it possible that I was so soon to meet some one of my old companions? It was to me a moment of hope and of doubt. My heart would leap and recoil, bound and then fall back again. The suspense would have been intense, had it not been for the thousand questions asked me by the curious crowd I was in. But right soon, while I was in the midst of an explanation, up dashed negro

Bob on a horse I knew as well as my brother. He was a most beautiful animal when I last saw him, a dark bay, round, up-headed, spirited fellow, and the sound of drum or band made him as proud and perfect a picture as ever was Bucephalus or Selim. He was quite a pet about headquarters for his kindness and tricks, and was ridden and lost by my friend Lieutenant Chisman. He had been much jaded, and looked thin now, and when I spoke to him, "Whoa, Frank," the poor animal looked at me so piteously, that I could hardly restrain a tear. He was caparisoned exactly as when I last saw him on the field of the Wilderness, with the same bridle, breast-straps, saddle-bags, and even the identical holster on the horn of the saddle.

Said I, "Did you catch anybody with that horse?"

Said Richardson, "We did, sir, his rider;" and, turning to his books, showed that it was recorded. There it was, in a heavy hand, "Homer Chisman, 1st Lieutenant, I. G. General Rice, May 6th."

It came to pass in this way: Soon after I left him on the skirmish line, to see the General, and perhaps before I was placed *hors de combat*, a rebel line of battle charged him from the rear. They had passed, unperceived, around the left flank. With a thousand rebel bayonets in his rear, he this time made a more desperate onslaught upon the rebel skirmishers in his front than ever, and this time not only drove, but went through them. Chisman, sticking to his horse, cried out to the subordinate officers to "rally on the center," but only about fifty out of the four hundred rallied, including seven officers. The rest were all captured on the spot by the enemy in the front or in the rear.

This party of fifty, now in rear of the rebel army, began wandering in that dense forest seeking our lines. They had little idea of the directions, and less of the positions of the armies. Two or three times, Chisman relates, they were within sight of the enemy's line of battle. Rebels seemed to be everywhere. They would go this way, that way, and the other way, and every time find in their front a force of the enemy. Night came upon them in their lost condition; but still they made another effort to escape. A line of the enemy challenged them, and because they would not, or could not, answer satisfactorily, fired upon them, killing two or three. After this, they selected what they then thought a covert place, and waited till daylight.

With the morning came the enemy on all sides; they had at last realized that a band of lost Yankees were wandering among them, and many came to the capture. By this time the number had been reduced to forty, and most of them had thrown away their guns in despair. They stood close together, waiting for the command to surrender. There was a roar and a crash from two sides, and nearly half of that gallant little band fell bleeding to the ground. Chisman, with his own hand, handed Frank to the man who gave him to Richardson.

It may seem selfish in one to say that, as much as I regretted the misfortune of my friend, I could not possibly feel sorry that it had happened. Misery loves company; so the first question I asked was, "would I likely be sent to the same prison with him," and being answered in the affirmative, I felt substantially better from that moment.

Here I found plenty of blue-coats. Hard by was a squad of about five hundred, and among them twelve officers. It was the general rendezvous of the army, and additions were being made almost every hour. I spent a couple of hours in conversation with Colonel Richardson, who was a very intelligent man, about politics and the war. From him I first learned, what I afterwards found to be quite a popular opinion in the South, namely, that a republican form of government is a failure—can not endure; and if they succeeded in the war, which they surely would, they would not continue six months a republic, but would make Lee dictator until they could select a regal family by ballot. As preposterous as this thing seemed to a Northman, this fellow, a decided leader among them, spoke of it in great earnestness and faith. In the evening I went down where the other prisoners were herded together, and looked carefully among them all for a familiar face. I looked long and thoroughly, but failed to find any one that I had ever seen before. But a "fellow feeling makes us wondrous kind," and I sat down with those strangers with great pleasure, until Colonel Richardson came down and invited me to his tent. Under the circumstances I went, not that I enjoyed his company, but out of curiosity more. It might result in something to my advantage; then, as I was a captive, I was inclined to improve my opportunity to study my enemies. I never could appreciate the bravery or good sense of a prisoner who would stubbornly and opprobriously hold out against those who had his life at their command. Captain Smith was one of those who, for the luxury of cursing the Provost Marshal, was tied to a tree all one afternoon. Private Williams, of Co. K 7th Ind., was another. He knocked a guard down and got away, but was recaptured while slipping through the picket line. Because he would not promise to knock no more down, they kept him handcuffed and under special guard for two days, when I prevailed upon him to make the promise and be untied. For my part, I accepted the situation and paid tribute to Cæsar. Nor did I lose anything by it that night. Richardson set me in the circle around his supper, and offered me *his canteen* first. It was here I saw the great Chieftain a number of times.

While we were eating, an old man, in plain dress, with

a single orderly, came riding by on a poor, iron gray horse.

"There goes the modern Napoleon," says one of the company, and he proceeded to tell how, at Spottsylvania, a few days before, he personally led a desperate but successful charge that had twice failed.

I have no wonder that the Southern rebels have such general reverence for Robert E. Lee. Verily, as rebels, they would be very ungrateful if they had not; for no one hundred other men did as much in holding up the Confederacy to 1865. Correspondingly, on the other hand, more widows and orphans should carry their tears and sighs to his door, and the ghosts of more murdered men stand around his bed at night, than any hundred others; for had Lee taken sides with the Union, the *cause* would have been *lost* in 1862, and 200,000 loyal lives saved. We were detained two days at Army Headquarters, awaiting the ingathering of a sufficient company to justify a guard South.

During the afternoon of the second day, we saw, far over the hills toward the army, a rushing mob, shouting, running, throwing stones and clubs at some object we could not discern. Towards our rendezvous they came driving, pell mell, and some concern about our safety was arising, when we distinguished, running for dear life, a lone man, with a thousand infuriated rebels at his heels, pelting him with stones. On they came, like a stampeding army, crying, "Kill him!" "Let me kill him!" "Give it to the rascal!" fell upon our ears. Now the mob is upon us, and the angry tide only staid by the guards' bayonets. The subject of all their brutality and passion was a poor, emaciated, hollow-eyed, defenseless Indian, whom they had captured and taken for a negro. The mob stood around our little camp, chattered and howled like so many ravenous wolves that had chased a lamb into the fold; they would not be satisfied nor retire until a committee of three surgeons had made a thorough examination and assured the motley mass that he was an Indian. The poor wretch had been chased for a mile, and so beaten with stones and sticks that there was scarcely a spot on his body that was not bruised. He belonged to a civilized tribe in Connecticut, and was a recruit to a Connecticut regiment.

We left Lee's headquarters for Gordonsville, five hundred of us, escorted by a squadron of Virginia cavalry. A day and a half's march brought us to the town. This was another step into the Confederacy, and another step into the knowledge of our enemies. We remained at Gordonsville over night, and till nearly noon next day. In the meantime the authorities here, to use an army term, "went through us"—that is, robbed us of whatever property we had that seemed profitable to them. By saying authorities, I mean a superior armed force, under the direction of a lame Major; and whether the business emanated from him, or a higher source, concerns no one now, for it is enough to know that we were called one by one into a small room, which had formerly, no doubt, been a grog shop; and while two *brave* men stood over us with fixed bayonets, a third, directed by the lame officer, made us disgorge the contents of all our pockets upon the counter. They even made us pull off our boots and socks and outer garments, and while the Provost examined the articles produced, the man examined the pockets to see whether anything had been left. They claimed to take nothing but what the Government furnished; but this they contradicted, by leaving anything with the private, and taking anything from the officer. In practice, their rule was to take from the enlisted man every woolen blanket they could find, and whatever other property they wanted. From the officers they wanted money and maps—the one would bribe guards, the other would facilitate an escape. The ivory-handled tooth-brush of Lieutenant Brown, a heavy artilleryman, was something "new under the sun" to the dignitary, so he threw it into his curiosity collection. So was also the silver tobacco-box of Captain Mahon—it would make a nice souvenir for Betsy Jane, and it was confiscated.

At Gordonsville we took a lesson in starvation. We had had nothing to eat since leaving Lee's army, thirty-six hours before; and many as were the promises of rations as soon as we got to Gordonsville, we lay around all afternoon and till 9 o'clock at night before they came. They were then as follows: One pint of unsifted corn-meal to each man, measured by the sack, and a mouthful of bacon to every two men. This was all they gave us. Not a skillet or a pot to cook it in, and not a splinter of wood to cook it with. We were all hungry—yes, very hungry; but our appetites were not generally sharp enough to take the raw, unsifted meal. Some of the men humorously insisted that the meal itself was all good enough, but the cobs and beans made it a little stale. So most of the meal was put in our pockets till we got hungry, and with our ration of meat in our mouths to encourage our stomachs we laid down to sleep.

Next morning we got nothing more to eat. Wood was promised every ten minutes, but altogether failed to come. The men were inclined to make the best of it. Few that I noticed were grieved or fretted. I only remember one old Irishman, from a West Virginia Regiment, who cried a little for his dear wife's sake—she would be so troubled if she knew how hungry he was. Much of the forenoon was spent in joking and talking about rich diets; but towards meridian I noticed that a good many had been wrought up to the taking of a little stall provender.

At 12 m., we were upon some open cars, and off for Lynchburg; and like Tom Moore, by London, were glad enough to quit "the dear —— dusty town."

Charlottesville lay in the way. This place, for pie-venders, is equalled only by York, Pennsylvania. Most of the men who saved a penny ftom the thieves at Gordonsville, spent it here. One prisoner had a five dollar greenback, which he gave to an old negro woman for a half moon pie. A rebel, seeing this transaction, demanded the money of the woman as unlawful currency, and to insult us as defenders of the government, tore it up into fragments, and stamped it in the ground. This was in sight of honored Monticello, and the wonder is, that the spirit of the mighty dead did not come out of its grave and palsy the hand that would so insult the government it did so much to establish.

Lynchburg, nestled as it is at the foot of the Blue Ridge, among spouting springs and countless shade trees, looked alluring enough as we rode up. The many steeples from among the trees, stretching high their necks, as if to look over the mountain; the historic James, at this point scarcely more than a brook, driving along at the south, together with the undulating streets, the antiquated architecture, and the little signs of war, created in us emotions quite hostile to the facts in our case. From the signs of freedom and comfort pervading the place, it was hard to believe that we could be in Lynchburg, and yet be captives. But a thorn was in store for us here, that goads me unto this day. Here, the officers, fourteen of us, and the men, were separated—the men taken to the Fair Ground, we to the Lock-up. If our captors had taken us around Lynchburg, I, for one, would have had a much better opinion of Virginia hospitality and kindness. The Lock-up was a miserable den. It was found in the upper story of a solid brick block, its north end facing the street. The place had been fitted and used since the war to confine not only criminals against the State, but deserters from the army, and at this time we found in it every manner of men. They lodged us in an apartment 20x35 feet, with but a single 2x3 window in the south end, that overlooked the sinks and back-yards of the street. To make the room as dark and dismal as possible, they had made a temporary board partition across the north end, thus cutting off a little room and shutting out the light and air from that direction. There were in addition to our number, in the same room, thirty others, of a heterogeneous, motley, mongrel tribe of criminals, some of whom, perhaps, had not washed their skin or clothes, or had a lung full of fresh air for a twelve months. As a matter of course they were all covered with vermin—so was the room These wretches were never taken from that room for any purpose. Everything they received was brought to them, and a row of halves of whisky barrels set along the blind end of the room to breed death among them. The place was a perfect Pandemonium—the inmates were as fearful to a decent man as an imp is to a Christian. No light nor ventilation, save what little came through the narrow window in the south. No stool nor bench, and the floor so covered with slime and filth, that we could neither sit nor lie down without getting besmeared. To lie like hogs in the filth was most revolting to us new arrivals. We kept astir till our legs became swollen, and as we took the foul, fetid atmosphere into our lungs, it seemed like the very shafts of Death. We would crowd around the little aperture in the south end for fresh air, but upon the approach of a haggard, pale, dirty, rancid criminal, we would disperse like he were a scorpion.

They kept us six days in this hell. In the meantime, we saw a relic of the "Institution." It was in the room cut off the north end of our apartment, and through some holes that had been bored in the temporary partition with pocket knives. A slave was brought in three times in so many consecutive days, and whipped. He had stolen ten postage stamps and a five dollar Confederate note, for which he was sentenced to receive thirty-nine lashes upon his naked body. It was executed thus: Three big men, one white and two black, would lead the boy to the room—he crying and begging. First, they would strip him entirely nude—then set him upon the floor and bind his thumbs and great toes together, attaching a rope thereto ten feet long. Now the white man would lay on the naked body with a cowhide, four or five licks with all his power; then the two negro attendants would seize hold of the rope and drag the fellow twice about the room, he screaming and piteously beseeching them. Now, another halt, another four or five lashes; another dragging about the room, and so on until thirteen lashes were given; and the entire round of the floor, every inch of it, was marked by the slave's blood. This was our six days' experience in Lynchburg, and if we left there without the seeds of death in our bodies, and a maniac fear of our captors in our hearts, it was not for want of effect on the part of the authorities to produce such a consummation.

Danville was our next point. This has been a pleasant country town of three thousand inhabitants, and had the signs of opulence. Three large cotton factories stand within a hundred yards of each other, and the massive piles of brick, as residences, bespoke a better past than we found present in Danville. We kindled no curiosity by going into the place. The cotton factories alluded to had been prison-pens ever since the war began. Disarmed Yankees were as common in this place as dewberries, and as we marched up town in the middle of the street, five hundred of us, if a single man turned to look at us more curiously than he would at an old blind mule, I did not see him. We were locked up in one of the factories and fed.

At this point our guards were changed. It was the line of Departments, and we were transferred from the Virginia to the North Carolina Department. We gained, perhaps, nothing by the change. Both parties had been too long engaged in the business of guarding prisoners to find any novelty in it, or be very kind or even-tempered.

Two days afterward we were again on the cars, billed for Macon, Georgia, the general rennezvous for Federal officers, prisoners of war, and the enlisted men for Andersonville.

Jamestown, in Guilford county, N. C., is a station on the route. Since our experience at Lynchburg, I had practiced as little ostentation in my captivity as was convenient. So, when we got to Jamestown, I was sitting in the back end of a box car. Our train stopped a few minutes on the switch until another train should pass, and while there some one came to the car door and asked if there were any Indianians aboard. Some one in the car answered affirmatively, and then turning to me, said that a gentleman (?) wanted to see me at the door. Guilford county and Jamestown are household words in many Hendricks county families. To me they were as familiar as the name of my own native village; besides, too, their close relation with many families in this State, and the many Friends residing there, had given the place same reputation for Union men. This reflection awakened in me the thought that I might find a friend, so I went to the door.

A man in gray, with perhaps some lace about the neck, and with a canine look, softly accosted me:

"Are you from Indiana?"

"I am, sir."

"What part?"

"Hendricks county."

"Ah! why it is from there I had hoped to find a man—and what part of Hendricks county?"

"Plainfield, sir."

"And your name?"

"* * * *"

"Is it possible? Why, I've eaten at your mother's house a dozen times?"

"Surely," thought I, "I'm in luck. If the fellow has accepted my mother's hospitality, he certainly will not deny the same to me, under these circumstances."

He hurriedly asked me questions about families in this county, but more particularly about one that had left considerable property in that State before the war.

"Were the boys in the 'Yankee Army?" he asked me a half dozen times, in as many minutes.

"Now, wasn't Taylor in the Six Months; or the Ninety Days' Service; or the Thirty Days' Service?"

A little suspicious from the frequency of his questions, I asked him why he was so much concerned.

"Oh," said he, "I just wanted to know."

"Well," said I, "if Taylor was in the Army, what would be the consequence?"

"Why, sir, I would confiscate his estate before night—that is what the consequences would be. We've already thrown Z.'s into the public crip, and the moment Taylor enters the Yankee Army, his goes too."

He proved to be a perfect land-shark, or its equivalent

—a tithing officer, whose duty it was to go about from house to house—as well to the poor as to the rich—with a squad of soldiers, and take by force, if necessary, one-tenth part of everything produced, for the government. The poor widow and the impotent was not even spared; but her tenth row of corn must be counted and her tenth row of potatoes, her tenth pound of butter, her tenth pound of yarn, her tenth yard of linsey, and her tenth of everything must be handed over to the *brave* officer, who was not "afraid" to punish her if she refused. This was the office of the man who "had eaten at my mother's house a dozen times," and was now eating at the lives of widows and orphans, and grew rich enough in the business to drive a flourishing hotel in Greensboro after the war. This scoundrel's name was, for short, Bill Reese. He not only had a mean object in view in questioning me, but tried to take the dishonest advantage of leading me into familiarity by speaking of my mother's hospitality, (which, by the way, I am glad to state, was all a fabrication; or, rather, he had eaten frequently at my "mother's house" in 1862, but not from my mother's table, but from the bounty of those whom he was just then seeking to injure). To prove himself more fully a consummate villain, as the cars moved off he insolently pushed away an old woman, who rushed up to give us something to eat. He has, however, now fully accounted at the bar of God, and should be forgiven in the minds of men.

On we went, via Salisbury, Charlotte, Columbia, and Augusta; it was at the latter place where we saw more signs of loyalty than we had before seen in the South. Here a family of New Jersey folks met us at the depot, where we stopped for an hour, and with a few others, exerted themselves to get us up a "square" meal. And they met with some success. The soft, white bread, sandwiches with boiled ham, butter, boiled eggs, and dewberry pies, did seem most delicious indeed.

We arrived at Macon about the 10th of June. Upon entering the suburbs of the town, the train stopped and put off the fourteen officers; then moved off to Andersonville with the enlisted men. To the left of the railroad, 300 or 400 yards, an ominous inclosure at once attracted our attention. The fence or wall, raised sixteen feet high, constructed very closely of heavy upright boards, and surmounted by a causeway, with armed men thereon at every twenty paces, sluggishly walking to and fro. Just before us was the gate, spanned from post to post by a broad, towering arch, showing in its curve, in huge black letters—black as the principle that wrote them there—"Camp Oglethorpe." This gate was neither brass nor iron, but was a ponderous affair, and before us had creaked behind thirteen hundred Federal officers, prisoners of war. Without command, we started for the pen, for we knew that it was our present destiny, and would be driven if we went not voluntarily; besides, notwithstanding it was a lock-up, we were right anxious to get inside, as well to see our friends we expected there, as to get rid of such immediate contact with the rebels. We were conducted first to the office of the prison, which stood but a few feet from the gate, and there halted and detained until preparations could be made within for another examination. It seems clear to me that during the last years of the war, the rebels were determined that no prisoner should retain any valuable thing; not even his life, if they could devise the slightest shadow of justification for taking it.

As thoroughly as they stripped us at Gordonsville, we were yet to be subjected to a more severe scrutiny at Macon. At Gordonsville, after search, we were permitted to go back into our company, and by slipping from one to the other, managed to save a few things; but at Macon, as fast as robbed, we were sent into the pen.

Everything being ready, we were called by turns inside. This time they even made us strip our vests and pants, and so ravenous were they for greenbacks, that every seam and double of our garments were examined with the greatest care. The few dollars that had been concealed up to this point, were turned out here, and for which the man in the sash executed and delivered a receipt with the utmost suavity; all the time, too, swearing about the Gordonsville Major stealing from us; that that was properly his duty, and nobody's else. These receipts were too much of a mockery for Captain Todd, of the 8th New Jersey, who at once tore his up in the face of the giver.

As we were examined and recorded, we were sent through the gate. Captain Eagan and Lieutenant Brown were the first to enter. And now followed something that I could not then understand; I should have had less trouble in the world if I had.

Immediately after the big gate slammed, some one inside shouted at the top of his voice, "F-r-e-s-h fish! F-r-e-s-h fish!" which was caught up all over the pen, and re-echoed by perhaps five hundred men. "F-r e-s-h fish! F-r-e-s-h fish!" still resounded within, and we could hear what seemed to be, and what really was, a thousand men rushing headlong to the gate, shouting those mysterious words. I, for one, did not like to hear it. It sounded to me like a very queer way to receive a friend in distress. So I decided that I would not longer fret to get in there.

"What's all that confusion in there mean, guard?" said a young Lieutenant at my side.

"Why, those are the old Libbyites, who have become

so demoralized and starved that they kill and eat every fresh man that is put among them," replied the guard," earnestly.

"No, they don't," most piteously rejoined my friend.

"I'll be d——d if they don't," emphatically retorted the rebel.

And what we could hear from the inside was by no means calculated to contradict this remark. Such ejaculations as "Don't kill him;" "Don't cut his throat with that case-knife;" "Oh, let him say his prayers;" "Oh, men, have some mercy—let his blanket alone;" "Don't take his coat;" "His boots are mine;" "His haversack is mine." Louder, "Put him on a stump," etc., etc., fell like hot water on our ears. We had less faith in going into that den than Daniel had in going into the lion's.

But our turn came, and with it we thought our ends. Lieutenant Smith Culver and myself were led to the gate together. We looked volumes at each other as the guard pounded the boards with the but of his gun. The bolt glided back, the hinges creaked, the gate swung open, and then—there appeared before us a sea of ghastly, grizzly, dirty, haggard faces, writhing and seething, this way and that way. As we stepped in the noise of the crowd within hushed. We were frightened near out of our wits. In we went—the writer in the re— —the Dead Line was passed, and sooner than I can te—, my comrade was swallowed up in the mystic mass. ome-thing like a thunderbolt came down upon my s' .lder, my blanket was snatched away. I was seize— — the arm, jerked headlong to one side, and somebod a low voice, said, "For God's sake, follow me!" I t the best I could, which was by no means a failure ran like a scared dog, and I, like his shadow—a l the crowd, across the pen, through the barracks, o' anks,

4

we went till we had reached nearly the other side of the prison, when, half crazy, I exclaimed:

"Chis! what's the matter?"

"Nothing, if you will follow me."

I followed into an old building on the east side of the prison, and, sitting down with my boon companion, Chisman, upon the sill, he told me how it was. But I learned it better by experience than he taught me. It all grew out of a mania for news. The starving of the mind is as infuriating as the starving of the body. Those who have never been prisoners will little appreciate it. Penned up in the middle of the enemy's country, active operations going on in the armies, victories being won or lost, the rebellion failing or gaining, friends being killed or promoted; and not a letter or newspaper—not a sentence or a syllable to give the tidings. The anxiety for news was almost distracting at times, for the dearth was not of a day nor a week, but of a month. The only reliable information that came to the prison at all, was brought there by the recent captures, and it is for this reason alone that such commotion arose among them when a new man arrived. The phrase "fresh fish" was a distinctive term used to distinguish the old prisoners—the Libbyites, who were called "salt fish"—from the recent captures. The cry was always raised whenever there was a new arrival; and then everybody ran to see who it was, and hear the news. The crowding was beyond description. As many as could possibly hear a word, would edge themselves about the speaker, and those who could not hear, being vexed and mischievous, would sing out such remarks as the above, to scare the fellow and make him remember his initiation into prison. I have often, too, seen men gather themselves, a dozen or two together, a few steps from one of these knots of listeners, and in concert go against them with a rush—suddenly shoving them, and many times getting the object of their interest under foot, and sometimes hurt. This was what was known among us as a "raid."

The first day in prison is the hardest of one's life.

Chisman, learning from those of my party who went in first, that I was at the gate, took a position and saved me from the ordeal required of the others.

This was my *debut* into a prison pen; and if I live to forget it, I shall either be crazy, or an old man.

Among the thirteen hundred prisoners I found many friends—three of whom were from Hendricks county. These last were all "salt fish," having been prisoners about two years—most of the time in Libby.

If Captain Milt. Russell's wife had seen her husband, with his long hair and beard standing, or hanging a "*little*" miscellaneously about his head and face, the points of which, from the direct rays of a Southern sun, were colored like the surface of a black sheep's wool in June; his skin, from cooking in the sun and over pine knots, the complexion of a smoked ham; his pants and jacket composed of three qualities of cloth, viz., blanket, Yankee blue and rebel gray; his hat wholly of Yankee overcoat; his shoes, ditto; strolling among the prisoners, begging for a chew of tobacco, or a pipe full—she would, in my opinion, have had scruples about her matrimonial judgment. She would, however, have felt better toward him had she known of but half the times he spoke of her and Sella.

There, too, was Lieutenant Thomas Dooley. He had been a prisoner long enough to grow a little morose, and was big enough, I reckon, to get the lion's share of food, for really his physical state contradicted the old starvation story of Libby.

Lieutenant Adair looked by odds the most forlorn of the three. His health had been bad, his patience worse, and had it not been for the encouragement of his friends, I fear he would have gone to his "rest" in the South.

There were, also, besides Chisman, my Colonel and Mitchell, the "man on the roan horse," and many others of my acquaintance. They all seemed "glad" to see me.

The prison pen at Macon was as comfortable as any I was at. It was located east of the city, on an inclined plain, sandy, and a small stream of water running through the south end, and had formerly been used as county fair grounds. There were probably three acres inclosed, in the center of which stood a large, one-story frame building, which had been the floral hall of the show, but was now the bed-room of two hundred men. We had shelter for the most part here; besides, some boards were given us for bunks. The water we never complained of, nor the wood, for they were reasonably plenty and reasonably good. But the rations were inexcusable. So much has been said and written already about what prisoners get to eat in the South, that I would not be excused in repeating it here, but I do not wish my reticence construed into disaffirming anything that has been told. It would be hard, indeed, to magnify the facts in the case. But at no other place in the South did I feel the teeth of hunger so keenly as at Macon. This much only will I say, that my mess of four could make but two meals per day, consisting of a pone of bread, made up of water and two pints of unsifted meal. A little rancid bacon was given us occasionally, and a few peas, say enough for a dinner, once a week. The only fights I saw in prison, grew out of the dividing of rations, and they were not unfrequent.

I am ashamed to tell how we did in my mess, but will, at a venture. We alternated in cooking, and when the pone was done the cook would cut it into four parts, as nearly equal as possible, then take choice, and leave the others to take theirs according to priority. By this method the cook always knew when his turn came. If there were peas to cook, plenty of water was added, and by the time we got the *hot water* drank off, the greediest eaters were full, and left the peas to the more moderate. This fact generally preserved an equilibrium in our *soup* dinners. To preserve order, the prisoners were organized into squads of one hundred, with a nominal Captain and Orderly Sergeant; this one hundred subdivided into squads of twenty, with a Commissary Sergeant; and then again subdivided into messes of four. By this means the rations and wood came first to the one hundred, then to the twenty, and then to the four.

The authorities at Macon called the roll of the prisoners in this wise: The Officer of the Day would come in each morning, with twenty guards, and deploy them across the north end of the pen; then all begin whooping and hallooing and swearing, to drive us to the south end. This being accomplished, some interval between the guards was designated as the place for count, which was effected by us returning, one by one, through that interval into the body of the inclosure.

Tunneling was a big business here. There were three of them under way at one time, and came near being successful. One was ready to be opened up the last of June, but to accommodate the managers of the other two, was delayed to the night of the 3d of July, when the others would be ready—the three affording capacity to let every prisoner out by midnight—and thus have an interesting time in Georgia on the 4th of July. But the treachery of an Illinois Captain revealed the whole scheme, and the rebels came in on the morning of the 3d, and deliberately took possession of the holes, without a guide. It is said that the Captain was promised a special exchange, and likely got it, for after the fact was learned by us, through a negro, the traitor was taken outside, and never appeared among us any more.

The manner of making those subterranean avenues was simple but slow. The beginning of each, at Macon, was under a bunk built a few inches from the ground. As soon as dark came, the boards composing the bunk were laid aside, and the work began. First, a hole three feet in diameter was sunk four feet perpendicularly into the ground; then from the bottom of this hole, the tunnel proper would begin, at right angles, two and a half feet in diameter, and pass horizontally along to the place of exit. The digging was mostly done with knives, but a spade or two figured in the business at Macon. The dirt was taken out in sacks, tied to the middle of a rope, which was twice as long as the hole, fastened to the digger's leg, by which, when he had dug up as much as a sack full of dirt, he would draw the sack in, fill it up, jerk his rope, and the man at the mouth would draw it out and empty it into another sack, or hat, or blanket, or whatever was available. The off-borer would then start, throwing a handfull occasionally like wheat, carrying a little to the spring, where there had been recent digging, a little to the well with fresh dirt laying about; but the most general deposit was under the old Floral Hall. At the approach of daylight business would be suspended, the hole covered up, the bunk replaced, and two men probably asleep on it when the rebels came in for their count.

To give an example of the inhumanity of our treatment at Macon, may not be amiss. The spring was within twenty feet of the dead line, and it was no violation of orders to go to it at any time of the day or night. A German Captain of the 45th New York, on the 17th of June, at dusk, went to the spring for water, and was just beginning his return, when the guard nearest the point, without saying a word, or having a word said to him, coolly shot him through the body, from which he died in an hour afterwards.

A written appeal to the authorities to investigate the matter, was answered by promoting the homicide to be sergeant, and giving him a thirty day's furlough. The reward was freely circulated among us, under pretense of the officer having crossed the dead line—to be an example of reward to vigilant sentinels, and a caution to indiscreet prisoners.

Notwithstanding the failure of our tunnels, the Fourth of July was by no means forgotten by the prisoners. Captain Todd, of the 8th New Jersey, somehow had managed to smuggle into prison a little 6x10 Union flag. Immediately after roll call, the "magic little rag" was unfurled to the breeze, and hoisted on a staff. In an instant the prison was in an uproar; every man's heart was shocked as if by a current of electricity. One poor creature, who had crawled about on his hands and knees for a month, with scurvy, leaped to his feet, and shouted at the top of his voice, "Hurrah for the Union!" Others, weighed down with grief since the moment of their incarceration, shook off their loads and cried out, "Three cheers for the Red, White and Blue." The excitement was wonderful. Two or three hundred men gathered around the little flag and marched about the pen, making the wall of the prison reverberate the echoes of the inspiring song of "Rally Round the Flag, Boys." Then they marched into the Floral Hall for speaking. A rough structure by one of the pillars of the building, called a table, was used as a rostrum, from which short speeches were made till late in the afternoon. And they were, too, of the most patriotic and radical order, interspersed always with some national air, sung by the entire company.

The rebels got a little troubled over this, and twice sent in a corporal's guard and demanded the flag; but these were only laughed at, and sent away empty. A third time the Officer of the Day came in with a squad of men and bore orders from the Commandant of the prison, "that that flag must be surrendered, peaceably or forcibly." Col. Thorp, 1st New York Dragoons, was speaking at the time, and turning to the officer, said—

"Lieutenant, be pleased to say to Captain Gibbs that the flag we are rejoicing under is the property of the prisoners, and that it will not be surrendered peaceably, and that the moment he attempts force, twenty minutes afterwards we will be burning and sacking the city of Macon." [Cries of "That's it," "Who'll do it?" "Now's the time."

The guard stood amazed only a moment, for when they heard such ejaculations from the crowd as "Kill the d—d rebels;" "Take their guns from them;" "Rally to the gate," they left the pen in a hurry, and it was the last time they ever demanded our flag, though its display was an every day occurrence afterwards.

Colonel Thorpe had the honorary command inside the prison, but his retort to the rebel officer of the day cost him his position the same evening, as will be seen by the following order:

       C. S. Military Prison, Macon, Ga.,
Special Orders, }   July 4, 1864.
 No. 6.   }

I. Lieutenant Colonel Thorp is relieved from duty as Senior Officer of Prisons for a violation of prison rules, and Lieutenant Colonel McCrary will again assume that position.

II. The same order and quiet will be observed on this day as on any other.

III. A disregard of this order may subject offenders to unpleasant consequences.

GEORGE C. GIBBS,
Captain Commanding.

My memoranda shows that on the 20th of July, while I was kneading dough in a camp kettle, I heard the cry of "fresh fish" at the gate. At this date I was "one of 'em," and without washing my hands or a moment's delay, I was off to the gate, but not soon enough to get a place near the entrance through the dead line. But from the spot I obtained I could see the three strangers as they came through the gate, and see that the youngest of them was my old comrade, Shelton, whom I left in the rebel field hospital, near the Wilderness. He limped a little yet, but his wound was nearly healed.

But right here let us stop and hunt up Chisman. He is to be closely connected with us through the rest of this sketch, and it may be of interest to the reader to know who he was, and what he was. I wish you all knew him as I do—then you would have more interest in my story. He was to me more than to most men, because we had slept together for nearly two years, doing duty the while as "Western men" on a "Down East" staff. Our relation had been the most intimate, and, as a matter of course, when we met at Macon we paired, perhaps a little selfishly, too. Chisman is a rare man—one of ten thousand—a companion for everybody; thirty years old, blue eyes, light hair, sandy beard, five feet ten inches high, and built like a prince. He was a great wag, conversed well, was quick in repartee, sung a good song, and told a most excellent story. He was famous in all his corps for these qualities. In the army, life seemed to him more a jest than earnest. He felt no care, had no trouble; and when his appetite was quiet, so was his mind.

"Sufficient unto the day is the evil thereof," was his motto; and "live well, live jolly," his practice. His heart was as big as a mountain, and the consequence was, had always a host of friends about him. He was also lucky. As a Mason, of considerable degrees, he had fortunately found a brother, both at Gordonsville and Macon, and was admitted into prison with a good gum overcoat and valuable gold watch. This coat he sold at Macon, to a rebel officer, for $100; the watch at Savannah, for $1,200, rebel money. Another one of Chisman's rare qualities is, that he lacks selfishness—he has not enough of it for self protection; so in prison, among so many needy friends, it was found necessary, in order to preserve any of his funds, that I be made his banker, which office I accepted, and "faithfully" accounted to my patron for a full half of his deposits.

Immediately upon our meeting at Macon, and the sale of the overcoat, we set ourselves about preparing "for something to turn up." With a $5 Confederate note we bought a pint of salt, and sewed it up in a little sack, at both ends, so that we would not use it; also, with another similar note we bought matches—just five bunches—and sewed them up likewise; then, with another, a quantity of needles and thread was procured, and for the most part sewed ditto; the three necessaries then sewed up together in an oil-cloth sack, and laid carefully away. With these precautions, if an opportunity ever offered for escape, we would not be prevented for want of preparation.

CHAPTER IV.

LIEUTENANT CHISMAN—OFF FROM MACON—GENERAL STONEMAN'S RAID—AT SAVANNAH—THE CURIOUS POPULACE—DRAYTON STREET—CHISMAN AND THE REBEL GIRL—THE PRISON—MAJOR HILL AND HIS GUARDS—HOW THEY TREATED US—FROM SAVANNAH TO CHARLESTON — THE THIRTEENTH OF SEPTEMBER—CHARLESTON JAIL YARD—THE BOMBARDMENT—UNDER FIRE OF OUR OWN GUNS—THE DESOLATION OF THE CITY—YELLOW FEVER IN OUR CAMP—CONSTERNATION OF OUR GUARDS—SENT TO COLUMBIA—INTENSE SUFFERING FROM THIRST—THE REBEL REFUGEES—THE CADETS—CAMP SORGHUM—AMUSEMENTS—RATIONS—AN OFFICER TORN TO PIECES BY DOGS—THE FINAL ESCAPE.

During the latter part of July General Stoneman got to raiding around Macon, and begat fear in the hearts of our keepers, whereupon they decided to send us further south. On the 27th of July five squads, of one hundred each, were filed out of the prison pen and put upon the cars for Charleston. Two days afterward another five squads were called for, and this time I was in the count. We were sent to Savannah, where we arrived on the afternoon of the 30th. As we were the first Yankees, armed or disarmed, ever seen in the city, a great curiosity was manifested by the citizens to see us. The afternoon was very fair, and the sea breezes had begun to shake the boughs of the live oaks and moss-grown pines, as we rode in and diesmbarked on Liberty street. Everybody was out to see the Yankees. Drayton street, through which we had to pass, was literally walled, on either side, with old men, women, and children, of all colors. I submit that we were not in a fine, or even modest condition for a public presentation; but since we had no will in the matter, we felt no responsibility for our appearance. The weather was very warm; besides, there were many men in the party who had been prisoners two years, and had no better clothes. Some had on nothing but pants; some, nothing but a shirt; others, a little of both; unshaven, hair untrimmed, bare headed, bare footed, dirty, and with kettles, skillets, meal sacks, rice bags, or bundles of old clothes in our hands; and this was the style we expected and did present to the aristocratic citizens of Savannah. We were formed in four ranks, and received by a fancy guard, and started for the avenue. But the crowd was so eager, it was found necessary to halt us until the guard and police could clear the street to the sidewalks. This being accomplished, they led us into the guantlet of curiosity, and as we progressed, a hundred little boys ran after us, hallooing and shouting, like they would follow an elephant through our streets. Rebel bunting and mottoes were everywhere. On poles and ropes, in the windows and hands of the women and children. Among the many, there was one young woman who, perhaps, had lost a lover by the Yankees, and wanted to show her hate; else it was love of ostentation that brought the blush to her cheek before the Yankees passed. She was a luscious creature; painted and fixed up like a candy monkey, and stood at the street crossing, in the front rank, leaning forward, flaunting her "bonnie blue flag" in our faces, with a satanic sneer. The indomitable Chisman came up, swinging an old blanket in one hand and a bag of meal in the other, and seeing the enthusiasm of the Miss could but remember the seedy condition of his pants, and turning himself rather unfashionably about, remarked with much gravity:

"Miss, if you've got time, I wish you would tack a rag on here," at the same time pointing to a place that evidently needed something of the sort.

We were shut up in the United States Marine Hospital grounds. The 1st Georgia Volunteers took charge of us. This was the oldest regiment belonging to the State, having been organized and armed in January, 1861. They had been at the front since the beginning, and becoming almost decimated, were sent home to rest and recruit.

Major, afterward Colonel, Hill took command of the prison; and I am compelled to say that he and his officers and men, generally, were gentlemen, if such are found among rebels; or at least appeared to be in contrast with the Macon authorities. These were old soldiers, and knew a soldier's lot and how to sympathize with him. Hill enforced strict discipline in the prison, but it was as much to our comfort and convenience, as to his. He gave us tents, and boards for bunks; also, plenty of rations—that is of meat, meal, and rice, the two latter in a surplus, which he bought from us at Government rates, paying in onions and potatoes. Besides, he furnished us with facilities for cooking—kettles, pans, and brick for Dutch ovens.

Our treatment at Savannah was as reasonable as could be expected, and during our six weeks' stay, not a single prisoner escaped.

The spirit of retaliation was up at this time between the two contending forces. Five hundred Federal officers were already under fire of our own guns at Charleston, and it was hither we were sent on the 13th day of September. There is no date in all the calendar of time that has been by me so much thought of, and so much hoped for, as the 13th day of September, 1864. No other date has ever been, nor perhaps will ever be, the subject of so many doubts, and so many happy anticipations; for it was the date that terminated my three years enlistment as a soldier—it was the date that my regiment was to leave the wall of rebel steel for the embraces of their friends at home. With these reflections to discourage us, Chisman and I, members of the same regiment, stepped sadly into an old cattle car, for Charleston, the very fountain of the flood of treason that had engulphed the entire South.

The night of the 13th we slept in the Charleston jail yard, and watched with delight the red streaks that followed our two hundred pound shells as they were shot forth from Batteries Gregg and Wagner, every fifteen minutes, and came screaming over our heads to a full fourth of a mile beyond.

This was a part of the famous siege of Charleston; this was in the late war at least one feature of uncivilized warfare—that of placing prisoners under fire of their own guns. Just across the bay, on Morris Island, between the two batteries above mentioned, was an uncovered stockade, in which were confined a thousand rebel officers, to be torn to death by their own brothers and fathers if their shell varied a little from its aim. The thousand Federal officers in the city were scattered about "as the exigencies of the service required." I must say, to the credit of General Foster, the Federal commander on Morris Island, that he seemed excellently well informed in the various changes of our localities. The Charleston papers complained bitterly of the police and City Guard, because they could make no explanation of the mysterious rockets that could be seen almost nightly, in different parts of the city, and more especially immediately after the removal of a party of Yankees.

General Foster perhaps could have given a better explanation than any policeman or guard in the city, for if a party of prisoners were removed into a locality directly under the scourge, perchance not another shell would come near; and in a few hours afterward, open up with terrible effect in the very place they had left. One example: Eighty-six of us were taken from the jail yard to the private residence of Colonel O'Conner, on Broad street, and while there, nearly two weeks, not a shell struck nearer than an eighth of a mile. A party of rebel officers for convenience and safety, took quarters within a hundred yards of us. We were removed about noon—the rebels remaining, and that night, while safety was thought to be brooding over them, a two hundred pound shell from Foster's guns came crashing through the house, killing the provost marshal and a captain instantly, and badly wounding a lieutanant. During our confinement there, of nearly three months, the only casualty among us was one man slightly wounded in the hand.

At Charleston I was more than ever convinced that "the way of the transgressor is hard;" that retributive justice, though sometimes slow of foot, is sure, sooner or later, to overtake us all. Charleston, in 1860, was the Athens of the South; not only renowned for its learned and great men, but it might safely be termed the parent of southern ideas, and southern politics, and southern institutions. It was a city rich, aristocratic, licentious and arrogant. In 1864 it was the Babylon of the South, condemned and desolated. The hand of God had written ot wicked Charleston: "And their houses shall be full of doleful creatures, and owls shall dwell there, and satyrs shall dance there."

The celebrated Mills House, where in 1860 the elite of southern society crowded the halls and parlors, was, in 1864, the barracks of a ragged garrison. And Meering street where, in 1860, the wealthy slaveocrats drove their gorgeous turnouts, the buzzard munched his carrion in 1864.

The great fire of 1861, that laid waste its fifteen squares, with the almost daily fires occurring during a two years' siege, had utterly destroyed much of the city, and it was at this time nearly deserted, save by the garrison, and a few pauper whites and negroes.

The yellow fever broke out among us at Charleston. This is the king of terrors to the southern people, and as he took hold on us with such determined fatality, they became much alarmed. It was among us five days in the city, and my recollection is, that out of thirty cases among the prisoners, not one recovered. The rebels shunned us as they would an infected house, refusing to come near only when their duty compelled them. It was with the greatest difficulty that the Post Commander could keep guards about us; and one fellow that I remember, who was driven to his post, was in a few moments seized with spasms, and carried away *in terrorem*. I verily believe, that had they been required to guard us forty-eight hours more in the city, we would have been abandoned. But the Commander, Jones, on the 4th day of October, succeeded in getting some cars, and away we went to Columbia, South Carolina, without letter or despatch, and fell upon that high place of treason, like a thunderbolt, and had we been all armed and commanded by Sheridan, we would hardly have surprised them more. The Provost Marshal, who seemed to be a pretty clever kind of a rebel, fretted and complained a good deal, insisting that it was an imposition to so suddenly send fifteen hundred prisoners upon him, without even a chicken coop or a dozen men at his command. He at first refused to receipt Cooper, the Charlestonian, for the prisoners, but after some altercations and some compromise, the matter was fixed up in such a way that Cooper should stay with his men and take charge of us until some arrangements could be made.

We were kept on the cars all night, and suffered most intensely from thirst. The door before, at noon, we were crowded, or more properly jammed, seventy men into a dirty cattle car, with camp kettles, coffee pots, greasy skillets, meal sacks, rice bags, old clothes, and such other appendages as are found with prisoners of war, at Charleston, on a scorching hot day, and not twenty men of the six hundred tasted water till six o'clock the following morning. At this hour we were taken from the cars and herded near the railroad like a drove of cattle, and our disembarkation was attended with about the same noise and confusion. Men were frantic with thirst. Some supplicating, some cursing, some threatening, made a din scarcely surpassed since Moses smote the rock in the wilderness, and the rebels took no steps to relieve us—seemed pleased to see it. Our suffering, however, was not long to endure, for Heaven, in its mercy, soon opened up a copious fountain, which drenched us without as well as within.

Here, as well as everywhere in the South, we could see the results of the rebellion. One side of our corral was marked by a half dozen or more box cars, which, becoming useless to the railroad, had been set aside. Each one of these old cars was tenanted by a family of refugees, most, if not all of whom, had seen better days no longer than two years before. The third car from the left attracted considerable attention by the plaintive remarks of one of its female occupants. She was a lady of intelligence, and free to talk. Her story was about this:

In 1862 she and her mother were living at home with her father and brother, in luxuriant ease, in the city of Nashville. They had a fine place on one of the fashionable streets of the city, and had never known what it was to want for anything. But upon the fall of Fort Donelson they, with many other families, took fright and fled South, to escape the dreaded Yankees, taking with them nothing but their wardrobes, as they expected to be able to return in safety in a month or two. But two long years had now elapsed, and they were still away, having in the time been tossed about from place to place by every Yankee gale. Her father and brother had both been forced into the rebel army, and her brother killed. All their friends South had become tired, and cast them off, and now they were driven to the embarrassing extremity of living in an old condemned box car, depending for bread upon the cold charities of an impoverished public.

Immediately upon our arrival at Columbia, a telegram was sent to Hillsboro for a company of Cadets, in school there, and in the afternoon of the same day about forty arrived and relieved the old Charlestonian Guard that was over us. These boys, having been chosen from all parts of the Confederacy to be trained for heroes, now in their Freshman year, more than appreciated their importance, or in other words had the "big head," as the common soldiers thought, for they hated them worse than the Yankees. They came down in their suits of fine gray cloth, fitted by the tailor, paper collars, blacked boots, and white gloves, not only to guard Yankee prisoners, but to teach the common soldiers a touch of science in the profession. They seemed to enjoy the recreation mightily, till the rain came on again in the evening, and collapsed their collars as well as their spirits; then they got mad at everything and everybody. One little fiend got so voracious for Yankee blood, so eager for a loyal life upon which to climb into fame, that he took two full steps from his post to drive his bayonet through the body of Lieutenant Clark, who was negotiating with a negro woman for a corn pone. Not even a reprimand for this wanton murder ever came to the knowledge of the prisoners.

No suitable inclosure could be found for us in Columbia, and we were marched across the Broad River, two miles south of the city, to an old barren field that had been abandoned fifteen years, and was now sparsely overgrown with pine bushes from ten to fifteen feet high. These bushes were our only wood supply, and with a few exceptions the second day saw their ashes scattered to the winds. This camp was large enough—probably six acres in all. There was no stockade, no fence, no water but branch, no shelter—not even for the sick, the first ten days. The well men never had any, only what they contrived with their blankets, etc. Around us here was a row of pins, standing fifty feet apart, and from twelve to fifteen inches high. The line marked by these pins was the famous dead line, which the prisoner passed at the peril of his life. Outside of this line, thirty feet, was the guard line, maintained by sentinels, fifteen steps apart.

Such was Camp Sorghum, at Columbia, where the rebels reduced us to a condition as nearly to the level of beasts as was possible for them to do. I would not wrong them much if I were to say that they did not give us anything here but air, branch water and room, but I will do them full justice and add, that they did also give us each, daily, a pint of unsifted corn meal, mixed with beans and cobs pulverized, and lots of sorghum molasses. I am faithful to the fact when I say that during the month I staid with them at Columbia, they did not give us one board or tent for shelter, nor one ounce of meat or bread, and if I will except a half pound of flour they gave us each two or three times, and a couple of spoonfuls of salt as often, then with the meal and molasses I have told it all. Not even a pan or a skillet, or a bucket, or a kettle in which to save our rations or cook them; and had it not been that a few of these articles were clandestinely carried away from other prisons, and procured

with private means, it is hard to imagine how we woul[d]
have got along. As it was, if we put in the count fla[t]
rocks, pieces of tin, scraps of old iron, etc., we had [a]
cooking utensil to about every twenty-five men. Th[e]
most valuable of any I saw in use was a slab of cast iro[n]
two by three feet, that would turn off at single bakin[g]
cakes enough for six men. This thing was kept in th[e]
fire nearly all the time, and accommodated more than [a]
hundred men. Meal for five, and once for nine days, wa[s]
issued to us at one time, and if it rained the next da[y]
we had our dough kneaded for four days to come, and [if]
it was sour for the three last days it was only our misfortune. We received our meal any way we could. Som[e]
were driven to the extreme of cutting off their pant leg[s.]
Others, more fortunate, got along by tearing the linin[g]
from their coat sleeves, or by appropriating a spare gar-
ment; anything and everything that could be used wa[s]
brought out on ration day.

To show how jealous those Southerners are of Yankees and Yankee ingenuity, I will mention that soon aft[er]
our location at Columbia, some prisoners got to diggin[g]
and scraping away in a bank near the branch, claimin[g]
that they had found a gold mine. The rebels, immediately upon hearing the report, contracted the guard lin[e]
so as to leave the gold mine outside.

Notwithstanding all the efforts of our captors to exter-
minate us and make us miserable—notwithstanding a[ll]
our destitution and exposure, good feeling prevailed generally among the prisoners I think more than at an[y]
other place—a more general disposition to be jolly, an[d]
a determination to hold out against the designs of o[ur]
captors.

The sorghum molasses that was given us in such abu[n-]
dance was the source of much merriment. Men wou[ld]
reduce great kettles full of it to wax; then take it a[nd]

ke wax figures of every conceivable shape; make it) balls and throw it at the guards after dark; make l hang effigies of rebel celebrities, and such like. And nes of all kinds were resorted to—some of science and ll, others of the most foolish sort. One I will men-1, that was as silly as it was full of fun. We called it zz. It went thus:

lometimes as many as a hundred men would gather mselves into a circle, set a "dunce block" in the cen- and referee at one side; then commence counting idly around to the right, and every number that is isible by 7, or of which 7 is a multiple, instead of pro- ıncing the number you should say "buzz;" as 1, 2, 3, ì, 6, buzz, 8, 9, 10, 11, 12, 13, buzz, etc., each man pro- ıncing but one number. Now, when a man called a nber when it should be "buzz" he was caught, and as enalty had to go to the dunce block in the center and g a song or tell a story. Any one who did not at once pond to the judgment of the referee, was ejected from circle, and his place supplied by some anxious by- nder.

This game, foolish as it may seem, produced many rs of laughter at Camp Sorghum, for there being ny men, with no attainments in either, their efforts, ler the embarrassments of the occasion, were ludicrous eed.

t was a dark night about the 20th of October that a of us stood wet and shivering around a fire near the id line, that Shelton, suddenly buttoning up his brown ns, with emphasis said:

'I will die here now, or go out of this."

Before any one in the company comprehended the re- rk, he shot like an arrow across the dead and guard es, and was lost in the darkness. A half dozen shots re fired at him, but fortunately none took effect. He was recaptured after ten days, near Charleston, and returned; but upon a second effort in November went through to our lines. He now flourishes in Rochester, N. Y.

The rebels were guilty of but few things more unpardonable than that of hunting down prisoners with dogs, as they would a beast. In all civilized warfare, there are certain rules of honor—among them, this one: that if a prisoner escapes he shall have all the advantage of his own sagacity, by having nothing employed against him but the sagacity of his guards. In the late war the rebels entirely ignored this rule by engaging every means against their prisoners—even to the perversion of the brute faculties that had been created for a good and noble purpose. They had a pack or two of these trained dogs at Columbia, which they tried to make as fierce and terrible as possible. They would keep them tied up through the day, and at evening bring them out upon the lawn before us to feed, twelve or fifteen, jumping and yelling, and howling around their master for their food. It was these dogs that kept more prisoners within the guard line than the eight pieces of artillery trained on the Camp; for if one should go out and the dogs find his trail, he was sure to be caught, and apt to be torn to pieces.

One night Lieutenant Barker escaped. He was out five days. A two horse wagon came rattling over the stones towards the camp. It drove over the dead line. Two rebels got in, and two stood by and lifted out the body of the Lieutenant. Life was still in it, but the gash in the side, and the horrible mangling of the throat and face, showed that it would soon depart. His Captain brother, bending over him, piteously asked:

"William, what's the matter?"

But a whisper only answered—

"Dogs—don't tell mother, Harvey, how it was."

Next morning, soon after daylight, they carried the young man a hundred yards to the west of the camp and buried him. This is all we ever knew about it.

CHAPTER V.

LIEUTENANTS GOOD AND BAKER—THE HOME STRETCH—THE FIRST NIGHT'S DIFFICULTIES — OUR ORGANIZATION — THE FIRST NEGRO—OUR FIRST INTERVIEW—CHISMAN'S SPEECH TO THE DARKEYS—THE SALUDA RIVER—QUANDARY AS TO ROUTE—OUR SECOND INTERVIEW WITH THE NEGROES—OUR DECISION — STREETS OF LAURENSVILLE — THE IRISHMAN'S SHORT-COMINGS—LOCKED UP IN A BARN — IN TERROREM — GOOD AND THE GANDER—MARTIN AND MOSES—SUMPTUOUS SUPPER—THE TWO CAVALRY-MEN—NORTH CAROLINA LINE—NIGHT AMONG OURSELVES—THE HOUNDS AT ROSS'S—REUBEN — CAPTAIN PACE AND HIS COMPANY AFTER US — REUBEN'S FIDELITY—COLLISION WITH CAPTAIN PACE—SALUDA GAP—THE GUARD IN THE ROAD—FLAT ROCK—INTERVIEW WITH REBEL SOLDIERS — HOW WE ESCAPED THEM — LOST ON A MOUNTAIN, STARVING AND FREEZING—THE CULMINATION OF SUFFERINGS AND TROUBLES.

Our number by this time had swelled to fifteen hundred, and to supply all our wants we got not a splinter of wood except what we provided ourselves with seven miserable old iron axes, and carrying it a quarter of a mile upon our shoulders. To get wood, a party of fifty men was each morning taken out of the camp to the rebel officer of the day, and there each required to deposit with him a written parole of honor, not to escape that day while out getting wood. Then they were turned loose with liberty to go half a mile from the camp without guard. It was something like freedom to get wood, and there was always a general rush to get on the detail. It was by one of these wood parties that we made our final escape.

The woodmen approached the camp from the west, and the guards along that side were instructed to suffer them to pass through the guard line and up to the dead line with their wood, and there throw it over to the prisoners inside; and were further instructed to be very vigilant to prevent parole men from crossing the dead line from the outside, and also to prevent any prisoners from crossing from the inside and going out through the guard line with those on parole.

The 4th of November, 1864, was a very bad day. It had been raining almost incessantly, and now there was quite a proportion of snow driving through the rain. The wind that drove it against our unprotected heads was from the east.

Perhaps not a dry thread could be found on all the fifteen hundred prisoners. Grouped together here and there around a little smoky, green pine wood fire, they sat wrapped in whatever clothing they might have, wet, cold, hungry and disconsolate. It was one of the gloomiest times I ever saw in prison; but a morsel to eat, and it sour and unfit for swine; winter approaching, and no shelter nor hope of exchange. Is it wonderful, then, under such circumstances, that men should say hard things against Secretary Stanton, and even Gen. Grant, whose responsibility we always understood was great in the suspension of exchange.

It was on this 4th day of November that I tired of yawning around a fire of green pine limbs, and to give my eyes a little freedom from the smoke, went sauntering around the camp. While passing along the west side, I saw a prisoner from the inside jump across the dead line, and go out and off with the paroled party. A ray of hope lighted up my eyes, and I hurried off to find Chisman.

I found him where I expected, sitting by a fire, in a perfect jam, smoking his briar-wood pipe of huge dimensions. He looked unusually forlorn. I never before saw him so much so—not a smile, not a word; and the only solace he seemed to feel was in the puffs of smoke that rapidly broke from his mouth. Eminent writers and philosophers tell us that this narcotic is a great evil to the world—a great curse; that it is an enemy to health, to mind, morals and economy; and that if it is not absolutely sinful, it is at least foolish in the extreme to use it. Without controverting the soundness of this philosophy, I may be allowed to give it as my opinion that, if the anti-tobacco ultraists had seen the force of it in prison, they would not yet plead "war to the knife, and knife to the hilt." I make bold to say that tobacco did do a good office in prison. It drove away despondency; it cheered the heart; it led the mind away from too long thought of home, and invigorated it to invention and resolution; and many a life-boat, loaded to the guards, would have gone under had it not been for the buoyancy of this weed.

Said I, "Chisman, come here."

"What do you want now?"

"I think I see a chance."

"For what?"

"To get out of here."

"Oh, I have heard enough of your chances."

"But come and see for yourself;" and we walked off towards the side where the men were coming in with wood.

The wind still drove the rain and snow, and the poor guards, old men and little boys, who were about as poorly clad as the prisoners, were nearly all standing with their backs to the east, shivering on their posts, while the parole men were passing and repassing the guard line without notice.

"Now," said I, "what do you think of that?"

"Well, I am ready for anything," remarked Chisman. "They can only kill us, and send us to ——, which will, no doubt, improve our condition, and I am ready to risk it if you are."

Our hands closed the bargain, and we started for our things. I have said before, that as soon as Chisman and I met at Macon, we prepared for "something to turn up." In addition to our Macon stock, we succeeded at Savannah in getting a sheet of tin off the roof of a dead house, which we gave to Lieut. Holman, a regular "down-east" wooden-nutmeg of a man, from Vermont, who took the tin, and with a couple of stones and an old knife, made out of it two as perfect pans as could be. They were 5x8 inches, and fitted so closely that they were proof even against hot grease. One of these pans was an accession to our out-fit. At Charleston we added a tin cup; at Columbia we stole a meal sack while the guard whistled "Bonnie Blue Flag," which not only made us each a haversack, but a towel, also. We had a few corn chips on hand, and hurriedly baked up what little meal we had.

We broke our design for the first time, to Lieut. Fowler, who was guard that day, (for, by the way, we had to keep watch over our things to keep our fellow prisoners from stealing them), and a few other friends, and with salt, matches, thread, bread for two days, and a supply of tobacco, we slung our haversacks and blankets over our shoulders and started for the scene of action. A few friends followed behind.

As we went along, Chisman picked up a chip, and said:

"Well, let the fates decide who shall try it first." Up it went—down it came—and it was my first trial.

We had not long to wait. A party of eight or nine men were approaching. I set out alone, aiming to reach the dead line, on the inside, about the same time they reached it from the outside. As they came up, I communicated some signs, that they might know what I wanted. They favored me—threw their wood over the line, then gathered for a moment in a knot. I glanced to the right and the left, but saw no guard looking in that direction. In a moment I was over the dead line, blowing and panting like the rest. My blanket was spread over my haversack and shoulders, and thus created no suspicion, for the day was so bad, that every man who had one, had it on. Two other men in my squad had blankets similarly employed. So I walked out, and away to the woods, without any rebel being the wiser. But my "last state was worse than the first." I was really more troubled now than when in the pen. There I was, out of prison, and without restraint; but to undertake a pilgrimage of two or three hundred miles, through an enemy's country, without guide or companion, to be probably recaptured and murdered, or locked up in some county jail in the interior, to suffer and die alone, without the knowledge ever reaching my friends, was a task so stupendous in its outline, that it was hard for me to find courage to even think of it. As I went to the woods, I met another squad going in with wood, and said to them that Chisman was waiting at a certain point to come out, and that they must assist him all they could. The very mention of Chisman's name, who was a favorite in all the camp, was sufficient to get the most earnest assurances that he should be aided.

When I got to the woods, I sat down upon a log, with my back turned towards the camp, afraid to look around lest I should see the party coming back without my friend.

My suspense was soon relieved. An elevation arose between, so that from where I sat we could not see the camp. Some one said, "There comes a man that looks like Chis." I turned suddenly about, and to my overwhelming delight, saw the inimitable joker raising the hill, with head up, and hand-spike on his shoulder, striding like a Weston, full fifty yards in advance of his party. This happened about 3 o'clock in the afternoon.

There were two of the parole party, Lieut. Baker, 6th Missouri, and Lieut. Good, 1st Maryland Cavalry, who, seeing how easy it was for us to get out, decided that they would call for their written paroles, go back into the prison, which would relieve them of their obligation, then get out as we had, and join in the expedition. They called upon the officer of the day, whom they found snugly ensconsed in comfortable quarters, reading the news of some rebel victory (?) and asked for their papers, saying that they felt too unwell to carry any more wood. Whereupon, the dignitary, instead of going with them and seeing that they were inside, as was his duty, and had been the custom, just handed them their paroles and told them to go back to camp, thinking, no doubt, that the day was too bad for anybody to be foolish enough to run away. The boys started in the direction of the camp, but before reaching it, they gradually changed towards the woods, where they arrived in triumph with their paroles. It took but a moment to destroy and conceal them, then they were ready to "come marching home." They had neither blanket nor rations, nothing but a few rags on their backs, and wills to escape. Good had been a prisoner twenty-three months, Baker, eighteen. A corporal's guard was passing among us every once in a while, to see that all was going right; and to escape suspicion, we spent the evening as industriously in the wood business, as any one out.

At 5 o'clock in the evening, when the drum beat at the camp, we went in under a brush pile, and those on parole went back to prison. I never will forget with what feeling Major Young said:

"Good bye, boys; be cautious, and if you get through, tell the people and the President how we are treated."

How still we laid. Not a hand or a foot stirred, lest some passing rebel might hear the noise and find us. The cold wet limbs, and the colder and wetter ground, chilled us to the very center; but we clung the closer together, and shook the time away.

It seemed an age till *tattoo*. Some of that age we were at home telling of adventures to our friends; some of it we were being chased by hounds; some of it we were being recaptured and dragged back to prison; some of it we were drowning, in vain attempts to swim unknown rivers in the night. A few minutes after the *tattoo* had summoned the guard to quarters, we crawled from under the brush with the utmost silence. Good and Baker came from another brush pile simultaneously. The night was very dark. Yes, dismally dark. Not a star nor a spot of blue sky anywhere, but over head was drawn a black mantle of heavy clouds; around us was night, woods, and a heavy atmosphere, which, combined, most perfectly substantiated the proverbial darkness of a South Carolina forest.

We four grouped together a moment to deliberate; whispered like thieves in a chamber, and soon decided that our object, for the first night, was to get just as far away from Columbia as possible, in whatever direction was most practicable. We started through the woods; nobody knew in what direction; nobody knew where; slipping along like spirits, on tip-toe, in mortal terror of something; stopping every minute to listen; starting at every rustling of the leaves; squatting down to hide from imaginary men; pushing each other forward to lead; and thus we went along for two miles, when we struck a South Carolina swamp. In, one man splashed, before we knew we were near it. What now must be done? Drive straight through? No. We had heard too much about the horrid snakes and aligators infesting them, besides seeing something of them as we passed from Savannah to Charleston. And we knew nothing of its depth or extent. We could not think of trying to pass it. The only thing to be done was to go around it; and to the right we started for a passage. Tearing through bushes, limbs striking in our faces, brushing off our hats, splashing in the water, slipping and falling over logs and big stones, was the unvarying business of the next hour.

Now, another body of water is found. Found, not by the light, not by the noise it made, but by the incidental failing of a stick in Baker's hand to find support. It was evidently more than a swamp—from the nature of its edge, it must be a river—yet, a singular one; apparently on a perfect level with the plain, deep, dismal, without bank or bottom, creeping along as noiselessly as we wished to do. We got a pole, in the darkness, and sounded, but the end popped up like a cork, without finding bottom. Next we struck a match, in a hat, and could see the light strike the trees on the other side, a hundred yards away. Sure enough, it was a river, and looked like it might be Styx. That river—who had a heart stout enough to try to swim it? It was not found in our company that night, and it was the only way to cross it. Then, of course, the swamp was wider and deeper here than where we first struck it above. What next? To take down the river would be to go back towards Columbia, we supposed. So we must either cross the swamp or go around it in the other direction. Disappointed, tired, and already disheartened at the prospect, we began to retrace our steps. On we pushed, as fast as we could, but with Herculean efforts we made but slow progress. On, on, on! I cannot say how far or how long we went, but we went as far and as long as we could. The night was about spent. The chickens in the neighborhood were heralding the approach of morning, and we were not three miles from Columbia, or two from prison. Still the swamp confronted us with all its portents. But something must be done, and done now. We must either get further away, or prepare to surrender—to not be over that swamp by daylight, was equivalent to recapture.

"I'll try it if the rest will," says one.

"I'm willing, if the rest are," says another.

"Well, I'm not afraid," says another.

"Let us go in," responds a fourth; and we stepped into the water.

The night was not near so dark at this time, the clouds had broken up and were flying across the sky, and the woods roared with the gale that drove the autumn leaves in armies by us. It was much colder, too—freezing now. My blood chills yet, when I think of my first hundred steps in that swamp. The water was from six inches to two and a half feet deep, having in it many old logs and limbs, lying here and there, upon a soft slippery bottom. The bushes and briars pulled and tore us at every step, but the chief trouble grew out of the thought that we were liable at any moment to be smitten by a venomous snake, or feel one suddenly coil itself around our legs, else to set our foot upon the slimy back of an alligator. But to say nothing of the briars and bushes, we got along well enough, and got through the swamp.

Now that this much dreaded obstacle was overcome, we felt encouraged and made better speed. The forests were not so thick, and it was now light enough to select our way. We pushed along vigorously—Baker in the lead, and he led us with commendable alacrity. A road was found leading through the woods, that had the appearance of being but little used. To make the better speed we took it to the right, almost on a run.

Our ardor exceeded our prudence. Without believing it possible, we let a wagon, rolling over the loose sand, nearly run over us before it was discovered. Like four quails we darted into the bushes and fell on our faces. The wagon stopped—men muttered a little—then got out and struck a light at the hind end. We raised upon our hands and knees, to see a muscular son of Ham approach directly towards our place of concealment, with a blazing pine-knot in his hand, stooping and gazing as he came; also, a few feet behind him, the light fell upon the pale features of, "not a degenerate son of his illustrious sire" —Yancy. Before they got close enough, however to see us, we raised and "went out of that" in a hurry. One trouble from this was the great fear all the following day that they would put dogs on our track, but there was nothing more of it to us.

Morning was now upon us, and the next thing to be done was to hide for the day. In this, our inexperience begat difficulties; we parleyed and we disputed; we actually quarreled about what we should do, and where we should go. One wanted this, another that; the third desired something else, and the fourth thought all three were wrong, and he right. It was not settled until broad daylight drove us to the side of a log, in a cluster of alder bushes. And here we came near freezing. With our socks and pants, to the knees, saturated with water from the swamp, leaves wet and frozen, and in this condition we lay down, with nothing under us, and but one blanket over us, and suffered most intensely from cold till about noon, when the sun came out and warmed us.

From our experience, up to this time, we all could

recognize that some sort of organization was necessary to successful escape—just as necessary, in fact, as discipline is to a regiment on the battle field. All that afternoon we spent lying with our heads together, by the old log, discussing and adopting in whispers the following plans and organization, which we never had occasion to change only in a few unimportant particulars.

One should be commander; and in this we should take turns; the term of office should be twenty-four hours, beginning and ending at 9 o'clock p. m. This commander's judgment should be final in all disputes. He should say when to begin our march, when to rest, and when and where to put in. His authority was supreme in all things, unless an appeal from it was sustained by a unanimous vote, except direction, concerning which he should consult the party. We were to march in single file, three paces apart, so as to keep the front of but one man exposed to the road—the commander in front—whose duty it was, among other things, to keep his eyes and ears constantly open to catch the first sound or glimmer of an object that might approach from the front. No. 2, three paces behind, to observe the same vigilance on the right; No. 3, to the left; and No. 4, to give his entire attention to the rear. If we were passing the road where there was woods or weeds on either side, and the commander saw, or thought he saw or heard a human being approaching from the front, he would turn his head to the rear and "*hiss*," gently, but sufficiently loud for the rest to hear him, then move hurriedly to one side, the others following hastily, preserving their intervals as nearly as possible, each to find a bush or a log, lie down upon his face and observe the most perfect silence. Thus we would remain until something would pass, or in the opinion of the commander he was mistaken; then when he would "hiss" again, we would all get up in our places, move back again into the road and be off as before. If we were passing through an open country where we could not hide, and the leader should see footmen coming he would turn back and "hiss" twice, then he would about face and take right back the road as fast as he could possibly walk. This he would continue until we came to a place where the commander thought we could hide, then again he would "hiss" and leave the road as before. Nearly all the persons that approached were footmen—mostly negroes—and our backward business worked to a charm.

One going along at night and seeing some indistinct object that he takes for a man, if it grows dimmer and dimmer until entirely lost to view, is apt to conclude that it was nothing but an optical delusion, or, at all events, hardly attempt to hunt it up. We never had any trouble in it. But if horsemen were seen coming then we would leave the road in any kind of a country. If No. 2, 3 or 4 should see an object approach in his jurisdiction, he would communicate the fact as above to the commander, when he would take charge of the movement.

We depended mostly upon the negroes for direction and food. We applied for their assistance nearly every night, in this way: Seldom before 10 o'clock at night, when everything was quiet, would we approach their quarters. All go up within two hundred yards, then two stop, a third go within one hundred yards, and the commander go alone to the huts. The negroes were remarkably familiar with each other and the country, for a radius of ten or fifteen miles. Really they seemed to be acquainted with every peculiar tree or stone, or cow path within that distance. Say we were among a lot of negroes to night, before leaving we would ask them to give us the names of a few of the oldest and most reliable negroes, ten, twelve, or fifteen miles ahead, or as far as we would aim to go that night. They were always able to give the names—being plain Joe, Jim, Jerry—as well as tell us precisely where to find them. They were very minute in descriptions—could generally give the number of the cabin in the row, the position from the cotton gin, pig pen, or massa's house—just the way to approach safest; whether there was any dogs, if so, how many, and how fierce.

There is not an instance on the whole route where we were misled by a negro's description.

Our leader would go to the cabin indicated, knock on the door till some one would answer from within, then call out gently, "Bob," "Bill," or whatever name had been given: "Come here."

The credulous negro always came to the door without further words, then the commander would pluck him out to the side of the cabin; and invariably, after the first few nights, the first thing he told him was that he was a Yankee, trying to escape from a rebel prison; that he had three companions near by; that they were all nearly starved; that our only hope of escape was through his aid; and if this was denied we would have to return to prison; that we could not rely upon finding friends with white skins; and that it was as much for his good as for our own; that he had brought this calamity upon us; that we did not ask much from him, but that he would see his friends, such as could be trusted, and ask of each something, just what could be spared and nothing more. A few words about where we should go to hide and to await the preparation of food, and the fellow would be off in perfect ecstacies to communicate his secret to the "colored people."

Generally, every adult on the plantation (house servants always excepted) would be notified that some starving Yankee prisoners were outside, which was enough to bring every one out of his bed, to gather his potatoes, ash or hoe cake, or bottle of sorghum. No lights were ever seen, and seldom any noise made while they were preparing their mites. It would take from thirty minutes to an hour to roast their potatoes and hoe cakes; and then they would begin slipping out to us, four and five in a party. Sometimes forty negroes, male and female, would come to us from one plantation, each one bringing something to give, and lay it at our feet, in the aggregate corn bread and potatoes enough to feed a regiment.

The third man went up within a hundred yards, in order to receive and communicate a signal from the leader if he should be captured while at the huts. In case of a capture by four, or a less number, he should communicate certain signals by exclamations; then it was the bounden duty of the other three to go to the house and give themselves up in the hope of finding an unguarded moment in which not only to relieve themselves but their comrade, but if he should be captured by any number greater than four, he should communicate other signals, warning his friends to leave him to his fate.

We agreed upon a story to tell in case of surprise, and each committed every part that there might be no contradiction, but the leader should do all the talking when it was possible. We were not to talk above a whisper, cough or sneeze when it could be avoided, nor group together in the road; but all conferences must be held in covert places. This was about our organization and "plan of campaign," and we solemnly pledged to each other that we would faithfully perform and heartily cooperate in them.

It was night when these deliberations were concluded, and although but five miles from Columbia and but three from prison, we saw during the day not a living creature to disturb us. The sky had cleared off and the night came to us bright and beautiful. It was Saturday, and soon after dark we began to hear in every direction the incomparable "Ya-hoo, Ya-hoo," and songs of the darkies going to see their wives and sweethearts. We had no idea where we were, and but little what direction from Columbia. Besides, we had not decided what point of our lines we would attempt to reach. Three were for any point on the railroad between Atlanta and Chattanooga, as most likely to be easily reached in consequence of but little rebel force. Chisman was for Knoxville, because he had more confidence in the reports of union men in Western North Carolina. However, it was agreed that we travel west the second night, and the following day reach a decision—so, off we started towards sunset.

We were soon out of the woods and into the fields, and were not long in finding a "big, broad highway leading down," almost in the direction we wished to go. Not far off, coming down this road was a negro, singing at the top of his voice:

"Massa don't know nothin', don't know nothin'—
Don't know, don't know."

We made up our minds before he reached us that he should know something. A conference with him could do us no harm if his race was as faithful as report said; and if they were treacherous and would betray us the sooner we found it out the better, as it was impossible to get through without their aid.

Baker stopped in a fence corner in the field, and the rest of us retired a short distance. That wonderful song came from a wonderful negro, who pitched it to that key, probably, to give notice to Jerusha, down by the river, of his coming.

His melodies were abruptly terminated when Baker accosted him:

"Good evening, uncle. Where does this road go to?"

"Down to de riber, sah."

"Where are you going?"

"Gwine down dah, sah."

"Ain't you afraid to be out so late at night, lest those Yankees down at Columbia get out and capture you?"

"No, sah. I'se not afraid of dem folks."

"Why? Do you think they are friends of the colored people?"

"Some say dey is, and some say dey isn't. But I'se not afraid of dem."

"If you should meet one in the road here, think you wouldn't run."

"No, sah."

"What would you do?"

"Nuffin; I wouldn't be afraid."

"Well, sir, I am a real Yankee myself."

"Is you?"

"And want your help."

"Does you?"

"I have three companions over there in the field."

"Has you?"

"Hold on a minute, Uncle; we want to talk with you."

"Oh, I mus' be gwine."

"Hold on but a minute. We wont hurt you. We're your friends."

"Oh, I'se not afraid; but I mus' be gwine."

The word "Yankee" had sent a thrill to the fellow's heart, notwithstanding his bravery, which made his heels so strangely light that Baker had followed him a hundred yards before the rest of us got up. Now he was harder to manage than before. To see four Yankees crowding around him, in the night, was too much variety for him, and he kept retiring, first to the fence on one side, then to the fence on the other side, we following and assuring him of our fidelity and friendship; he in turn assuring us, with resolute zeal, that he "was n't a bit afraid;" in which, if he adhered to the truth, his actions most grossly belied him.

But the fellow was like all others of his race we afterward met, easily flattered and credulous, and when we once turned the key to his heart he was as completely in our service as if he had been a brother.

Ten minutes afterward we had gained such confidence from the boy, that he was planning what we should do, and where we should go to receive the colored folks from Beck's plantation, down on the river.

We went a half mile along the road with the boy, then he led us across the fields, around a hill, and into a grove in the rear of a long row of cabins. Hither he soon conducted not less than twenty negroes.

This may seem to many a reckless adventure, so soon after our escape; and perhaps it was, but it then seemed to us unavoidable. Trusting our secret to negroes, we felt was an experiment that must be tried, or it would not have been; for, much as we had heard about the fidelity of the blacks, none of us then felt quite willing to risk his liberty, if not his life, in their hands. But we knew nothing of the topography of the country, nothing of the rivers and roads, and had hundreds of miles to go in the night time, without compass, guide, or map; we could get no information from the whites—we must have it from the blacks.

Nearly every one brought us something to eat; a piece of corn bread, a yam, or a bottle of sorghum. They were a little shy at first, but our hand shaking and familiar address soon brought them into nearness.

This first conference was, in the main, like all subsequent ones, and can not better be described than by citing the old illustration of William Penn's treaty with the Indians. Only there were four of us, and each had his group sitting on the ground about him. As one old woman came up, we arose and shook her hand, she at the same time asking:

"Now, is you Yankees?"

"Yes."

"Do Massa Linkum want to free us cullud fokes?"

"Yes."

"Well, de Lod bress him; I allus thought so."

This, at the time, greatly impressed and surprised me. I was glad to hear it, for I did not believe that this light of liberty had then shone in the interior of the South. But "truth is mighty, and will prevail." It was no matter how the rebels might practice their artifices and their strategems; they might be ever so vigilant and cautious, yet it was not within their power to withhold from even the ignorant slave in the interior so important and necessary a result of the late war.

As an example of the means resorted to by the rebels to keep the slaves in ignorance and fear of the Federal army, I will only mention some of the stories told by this first party;

First. Their masters had told them that the Yankees were fighting to take the negroes from their masters in the South, to enslave them again in the North where they would freeze to death.

Second. The Yankees were trying to catch them to sell them to Cuba for sugar.

Third. That the Yankees wanted them for breast works in the army; that they would tie them together, men and women, and drive them in front of their white regiments to battle.

Fourth. That the Yankees frequently shot negroes out of their cannon, for disobedience, and would punch out the eyes of those who would lie down or try to get away in time of battle.

Of course they did not generally believe these stories or they would not have seen us on that night.

A rod to the left of where I sat with my auditors was another group, evidently more pleased and interested than mine. I think the principal part were blooming maidens, who shook their lusty sides and shoulders around Chisman, whose discourse was so ruinous to mine. The tittering of his crowd, and frequent outbursts of laughter, suppressed with both hands, were eminently embarrassing to my sedate remarks, for my congregation fell away, one by one, till I had not a listener. Then I followed, and leaning against a tree heard Chisman on the Emancipation Proclamation. I noted in substance the following:

"There is not one of you a slave now, if you only knew it. Mr. Lincoln has declared by that proclamation that the colored people are free everywhere, and he has called soldiers enough into the army to stretch around the State of South Carolina, and compel your masters to let you go. [Tittering.] Thousands and thousands of your race are already free. As soon as they get to the northern soldiers they tell them to go free, to do what they please, to go where they please, to work when they please, and for whom they please. And they go to work and earn lots of money, five dollars a day, some of them; and they get it themselves every cent of it; and they buy fine clothes, and great big high hats; and the women have fine satin dresses and parasols; they have fine horses and buggies, and drive headlong through town, splashing the mud on everybody. [Snickering.] Then, when Mr. Lincoln finds an old colored person who can't labor, he gives him a house, feeds him, and cares for him. Why, there is a place close to Washington, where Mr. Lincoln has built houses for, and is feeding and caring for fifteen hundred old and crippled colored people. Then, too, we have some rebels in the North, who don't want you to get free; and when Mr. Lincoln finds one of these men, he takes his land from him, and his horses, and everything he's got, and gives them to the slaves who run away from their masters, and I'll bet you'd laugh to see the girls swell when they get to thumping away on his piano. [Spasmodic laughter.] And it's all a lie about you having to go into the Federal army. The rebels tell you this to scare you. You don't go in unless you want to. They won't let the girls go in at all, but have them go back in the country and work in houses altogether, sewing and making clothes for the boys in the army; and they get paid for it, too.

"All the colored boys that want to go into the army to fight their old masters, Mr. Lincoln hires them to go; and he gives them all the nicest clothes, every one just alike; he gives each one a pair of new shoes, and a pair of blue pants, a fine blue cloth coat with brass buttons all up before, and great big brass things on the shoulders, and a new black hat with a brass eagle on each side and a yellow cord around it, with tassels hanging down behind; and the prettiest new guns—why, they are as bright as a new dollar, and have great long spears on the end to stick the rebels with. They are not a bit like the old rusty things you see the rebels have. And they are the proudest fellows you ever saw when they get their new clothes on, and their guns and white gloves, and stretched out into line. Then it would do you good to see them fight in battle. They just won't be whipped. They just raise the yell, and go at the rebels, and never stop shooting and sticking them until they run them every one. And they sometimes capture their masters. Once, in the army, a colored boy caught his master, and had him for a prisoner. The master thought that because the boy had once been his slave, he would not mind, and refused to go when the boy told him to. This made the boy mad, and he snatched up his gun and was going to shoot the old fellow, but he begged so that he didn't, but made his old master go back to his tent and black his shoes [tittering] and chop wood enough to get his dinner with. [Renewed tittering.] He then left him with the other prisoners. And they make officers out of the colored men, who have nothing in the world to do but stand around and tell the other soldiers what to do. Why, they say they have got one over in Tennessee who rides a horse and commands fully ten acres of men." [I think the last remark was suggested by a story told of General Logan.]

"If I were one of you I would never work another day in the fields, under your master's lash, but I would leave here before sun rise, and take every colored man and woman with me I could. Why, it's a shame to have to work as I know you do, and get no better food and clothes. We Yankees in the North do better by our hogs and horses than your masters do by you."

Afterwards, when I suggested to Chisman the doubtful propriety of such inflammatory stories, he turned to me sternly and said:

"This is no time for your moral lectures, old granny; I'll hear none of them till we get home. We must have these darkies for us, and I intend they shall be."

I never doubted the success of Chisman's policy, but there was one thought connected with it that created some uneasiness in my mind. It was this:—If the rebels should recapture us, and find out that we had been guilty of such incendiarism, they might take our lives in consequence of it.

We not only advised, but asked advice of those negroes in turn. We broke to them our notion of trying to reach our lines in Georgia, which they unanimously opposed. They urged that it would not do at all. The country was not only full of swamps in that direction, but there was the Savannah river to cross, and "Hood's big army," and worse than all else, the colored people in Georgia would not be our friends.

"Dey is all Secesh ober dar."

"Yes, said an old man they called Abraham, "youens had all better go to Knoxville, dey is no big armies up dat way, and de colored folks am all for de Yankees; an' I was up to Newbury de tnder day, an' I heard de white folks talkin 'bout de tories in Noff Carlina, an dey meant by dat dat dey were for de Yankees."

This conference took place a quarter of a mile south of the Saluda river, which proved to be that mysterious stream we had met the night before, four miles nearer Columbia, and we gladly accepted the proposal of these people to cross the river here in their canoes, as it would be to cross somewhere on either of the routes—Georgia or Knoxville.

Before leaving our new acquaintances we had them so thoroughly convinced that we were in good faith their friends, and desired to do them good, and make them free, that we had their entire service at our command. When we started to the river, they followed, and when we wished to hurry, they wished to detail a load of grievances, which became more burdensome as the hope of relief brightened. We were an hour in getting to the river. It was starting and stopping, talking and listening all the way, and even when we got to the river, and the oarsmen were impatiently holding the boat to the bank, some of them still hung to us to hear us tell something more. Every brass button that could be spared from our clothes was cut off and given them as souvenirs.

Two big burly fellows were in the canoe to row us over, and as many more would have gone if we had permitted. A few united strokes shot us to the other side like a dart. The boat was tied up to a log, and the two negroes went with us a mile and a half to show us a road in the right direction.

We found the road, we received directions, and parted with our friends.

Now we made good use of our legs till morning. We were encouraged beyond all expectation; our first adventure with the negroes had been a succes. We had plenty of rations for two days, and in our minds was some idea of the country and distance.

It was after midnight when we left the river, and we must have gone not less than fifteen miles before 5 o'clock in the morning. We kept the road, but passed near no houses if we could conveniently go around them. Two or three packs of hounds, an appendage found to nearly every important plantation in Georgia and South Carolina, were stirred up during the night, but made no savage demonstrations.

As soon as the chickens began to crow and lights to appear in the windows, we turned to hide in the thickest woods we could find. The leaves were just falling from the trees, and we effected our concealment in this way: As soon as it was light enough for us to see, we would select a secluded spot in the woods, gather a few leaves into an old tree top, or among some logs; spread one blanket over the leaves, put all our things under our heads for pillows; then lie down together on the blanket, and spread blanket number two over us, covered it with leaves, our heads and all, leaving but a little hole to breathe through. In this manner we slept when we could, and listened when we could not. It may contradict nature, but I will venture the remark that for the first four days and nights out of Columbia I never slept one moment; and the rest of the party slept but little if any more. So intense was the excitement, so painful the suspense, so distracted was the mind upon subjects of escape, of recapture and of home, that sleep could not find lodgment. We had not fully made up our minds what route we would take. The negroes had greatly discouraged us in our Georgia route; also between us and Knoxville lay two great ranges of mountains, which we could not cross upon the roads, and if a snow fell upon them we could not cross any other way, and it was already well into November. For further advice we called upon some negroes the third night, in the manner before described. We found these negroes just as magnanimous, just as credulous, and to our surprise of the same opinion about the safest and most practicable route to take. They re-affirmed the stories of the loyal whites in North Carolina and of the disloyal blacks in Georgia. This conference cleared up all doubts, and when we left there our faces and minds were towards Knoxville, taking direction at about forty-five degrees from the North star, when it was possible to have that guide.

Twenty-three miles were now between us and Columbia, and we had less fear and more hope.

For the next three days and nights nothing worthy of special notice transpired.

On the seventh day a little incident occurred that would probably be to our credit to omit, but trusting this sketch will come to the perusal of none but liberal persons, who will only look at these events by the light in which they occurred, and who will graciourly admit the circumstances to extenuate what, abstractly considered, would seem grossly wicked, I proceed to give it.

It was at a point between Newberry and Laurensville, and as was our custom we went into concealment in the forest before daylight. This time we had chosen a hickory tree-top that had broken off half way up while the leaves were on, and which still hung to the boughs. The trees and bushes seemed thick enough around, and had every appearance of being a good place to hide. So we crawled under its branches, spread out our blankets, sprinkled on leaves and went to sleep.

It was after sun-up when the first one awoke, and there, to the great bewilderment of all, within six feet of our heads ran a beaten path. It had the signs of considerable travel. What must be done? What could be done in safety? To be seen in South Carolina by a white man was to be caught—we felt certain of that. Here hounds were found at every mile, and trained to the business of hunting down men. To get up and move through the woods in broad daylight, was an exposure not to be hazarded; and to lay there by that path seemed one but little less. We were in a painful dilemma, and while we lay there debating in a whisper what we should do, Good whispered with an expression too full of meaning:

"Oh, my God! look."

In a second every eye darted to the South, and there within fifty yards of us came a white man along the path with a gun upon his shoulder. No time to consult, no time to cover faces, no time to resolve—he was upon us in an instant.

Few persons can realize our feelings. There we saw the end of our liberty within six feet, and but a single look, a single glance, and it would slip away. Heaven never read more thankful hearts than ours when he passed by without seeing us. He was an old man, and his eyes perhaps a little dim, or his mind might have been more upon squirrels than Yankees, for he carried one in his hand, and chased another before getting out of sight. He gave us such a fright that we could not think of leaving the tree-top to hunt another place, and be seen by squirrel hunters or somebody else; neither could we think of sleep any more that day, for much as we tried by turns, the thought of our miraculous escape and the possibility of another such peril, entirely overcame our efforts. We lay in great suspense, wishing for night and watching for men. About the fourth hour in the afternoon, which seemed to us about the fourth day, Baker turned his head from the north, and nervously whispered:

"Boys! boys! what will we do? I see that same man coming right back this path."

This time he was a considerable distance off when first discovered, and we had time to think and determine. After he had passed in the morning we discussed his case fully, in the light of his having seen us, and unanimously agreed that it would be a desperate case, and required a desperate remedy. We might swear him and let him go, we might beseech him, we might threaten him, we might force him to stay with us till night; yet, in either case, he might and probably would put a pack of hounds on our track in an hour after his release.

I never shall believe that it emanated from a bad heart when Good observed:

"Dead men tell no tales."

"Shall we do that if he sees us?" came hesitatingly from Baker.

"Do what?"

"That which Good spoke of this morning."

"Is it the safest thing?"

"Yes."

"Then, let us do the safest."

"What with?"

"His gun."

"Shoot him?"

"No; strike him."

An innocent man's blood was a heavy load to carry through life, but the horror of rebel prisons, and the hope of liberty and home, surmounted all other considerations, and we were wrought up to the terrible thought of sending the old man to "that undiscovered country from whose bourne no traveler returns," if he were so unfortunate as to discover us. This time we had the leaves better over us, and thrice happy for us and for him he again passed us by unheeded.

The boldest thing we did during the trip was to pass through the streets of Laurensville. We were on a road leading to that place, and struck a stream of water running through its suburbs. In the darkness it appeared like a considerable river. We wandered up and down its bank to find a canoe or some available stuff for a raft, without any success. We were all cowards when it came to the black portentous waters of an unknown river. Down below the ford some distance we found a railroad bridge on high trestlework stretching over the stream. It appeared to us that the only way to get over was to cross on that bridge or swim, and as we did not like the latter we started to do the former after listening fifteen minutes for a guard. It was 2 o'clock in the morning, and everything in silence and slumber when we crawled on hands and knees over the bridge and into the edge of town. Now, thought we, it will be just as perilous to go around the town as to go directly through it; besides, if we go directly through we can keep our road, which we may have much trouble to find if we leave it. Off we started, one after the other, reaching out for dear life, in the middle of a street covered with loose sand, making no more noise than four cats. A lamp was burning at each street corner and in many of the business houses. These lights were vexatious, but the most embarrassing feature was the short legs of Lieutenant Good whose Finigan lordship was illy adapted to pedestrian matches, and who unfortunately held the position of No. 2 in the march. He was as willing as could be desired, and his strokes as

7

frequent but his measures were vastly inadequate to the occasion. No. 1 rapidly extended his interval and Nos. 3 and 4 closed theirs as soon and were then unkind if not cruel enough to take advantage of their longer legs and transpose the vigorous Irishman to the rear.

But we got through the town of four thousand inhabitants, without any serious difficulty. Almost in the suburbs of the town, and just after resuming our proper places, we came upon a half dozen persimmon trees, loaded to the ground with ripe fruit. Our attention was called to them by their delicious fragrance, and I, being in the rear, could not forego the pleasure of stopping to jerk off a few in my hat. Chisman, in the lead, was enraged at my disobedience, and came hurrying back with uplifted cane to drive me to my place in line, averring the while "that nature made a great mistake in my creation, by not providing me with the grinning face and sleek tail of an opossum, to have had supreme delight in eating persimmons." I never thought so.

Two or three nights after leaving Laurensville, we got into another dilemma. Good turned out a negro man from his sleep at ten o'clock at night, and brought him out into a corn field for a conference. We told the fellow our whole story with its usual plaintiveness, but somehow it failed to arouse the ordinary enthusiasm in him. He heard our story without any emotion—said his master was very hard on them, did not give them enough to eat; beside, "Massa would cut his head off, sure, if he ever found out that he had given Yankees aid."

This was the first time we had met with discouragement from the blacks, the first time they had not manifested pleasure in helping us; it was a time, too, when we needed it more than usual. I believe we were entirely out of provisions.

After much flattery for his prudence and caution, we prevailed upon him to promise to get us up something to eat. But we must leave that field and let him hide us as he chose. This we did not hesitate to do, for the negroes had been so uniformly faithful that we had no doubts, and only said to him lead the way. Off we started, slipping through the corn and over fences, till we reached the barn-yard. We had never been hidden about buildings before, and such a retreat was not altogether harmonious with our ideas of safety, yet it must be all right in a friendly negro, and when he unlocked and opened the door to a log barn we followed him in without a question.

The first floor and our apartment was stuffed full of unbaled cotton, excepting a little space near the door, and the man requested us to lie down here, and be perfectly quiet until he came again. He then went out, shut the door and went away. The cotton was so soft, so bed-like, that we all went to sleep, took quite a nap, woke up, and the negro had not yet returned. Suspicion began to creep upon us. What could delay him so long? Surely he had been gone an hour, and that was enough. We listened, we whispered, we pulled our way through the cotton to the cracks in the barn, looked out, saw nothing, heard nothing. We were not more than three hundred or four hundred yards from the master's house, and there was a light in the window, while every negro hut was as dark as the night. Could it be possible that the rascal had either abandoned or betrayed us? and yet we could imagine no excuse for delay. If they had nothing to give, why did not he return to report? if they did have to give, they had plenty of time to prepare it.

Our own philosophy frightened us, and all decided to leave the barn and negro at once. We put on our accouterments, picked up our sticks, and were ready for the march, tried to open the door, and—"Ye Gods!" it was locked on the outside.

"No, no!" said two or three voices at the same time, "it is not locked—he only closed it."

In an instant we were all pushing at that door like it was coming to crush us. Why we were so frenzied, why we crowded each other so to get "my strength against it," or why we did not combine our strength against it, I can give no reason now; but there was such distraction, such individual resolution to get out of that prison, that all reason was blind, and we crowded around that door, pushing and accusing each other; then diving into the loose cotton to the wall, hunting some hole for escape; then on top against the loft, and with back and shoulder lifting with all force at the boards loaded heavy with hay; then back to the door, and accusing another of being guilty of knowing the fellow locked the door, or of thinking the negro treacherous, without expressing himself or something else. Each one felt that some one was responsible, or ought to be, for us getting into the trap, while the truth was we all went in without a suspicion. We were "taken in," beyond all doubt. The door was locked, and for what purpose! Certain to keep us there until he returned again, and if he intended to return as a friend why deem our confinement necessary. The case seemed clear, he had locked us there in that stronghold till he could gather force enough to capture us. Oh, but if we ever got out of that barn safely, we would never trust another negro; no, indeed, we would shun them hereafter as we would the rebel army.

It seemed fully an hour after our suspicions were aroused before we heard footsteps approaching the barn. Tramp, tramp, tramp they came, a half dozen of them, with dogs growling around. Our hearts leaped to our mouths—the leader faintly whispered, "Shall we fight them?" and noby answered, but we trembled from head to foot as the rusty lock creaked outside. We stood ready to be delivered when the door swung back. Open it came and in stalked Joe, with four other black men, armed to the teeth with——corn bread and roasted sweet potatoes. Joe was acting in good faith all the time, and tried to explain his absence by saying that there had been a light in his master's window, and that they could not safely proceed with their cooking until the white folks were all in bed. I think however, after all, from Joe's manner of conversation, that it took him about all the time to stir among the negroes and get back. We felt so good when we learned that the fellow had not been false, that we did not even scold him for the scare he had given us; besides he had made considerable amends by the good quantity of excellent potatoes. However, we left there that night, firmly resolved never to get into such another snare, even if negroes did propose it.

The first several days out our principal want was meat. We could get almost everything else from the negroes we needed in sufficient quantities, but of meat we got none of any kind, from the fact that they got none themselves, nor had they, as a general rule, drawn a mouthful from their master's larder for two years, in consequence of the demand of the army. Our systems very much needed meat. Our appetites, their spokesmen, cruelly teased us night and day for something to supply muscle. To meet this demand we, two or three times, visited hen-roosts with "felonious intent," but were every time disturbed by disturbed dogs, and out of distinguished respect for the rest and quietude of these quadrupeds, we forbore any further enterprises of that sort. But a capital idea struck Good one night, as we came upon a flock of geese sitting in the road in their slumber.

"Say, boys! let's have a goose for to-morrow."

Why we could almost taste the savory "sentinel of Rome" in the very words as Good spoke them. Certainly, everybody was agreed, and the leader led back the road a piece to prepare for capture. They were sitting so close to a house that the leader thought it safest for us to drive them up the road out of hearing of the folks. So at it we went, whispering "shew, shew, shew," but the offended family, instead of walking quietly off at command, set up an uproarious "hut, tut, tut, tut," which succeeded in repulsing us completely. We fell back a few rods for another council. Leader this time said we would walk up abreast and simultaneously fire a volley of clubs into their ranks, and surely some one would bring down a bird. Our walking sticks were the very things, heavy enough to be deadly, and they were used. Whiz went the canes—slam against the fence one or two of them, and off went the geese, noisy as before, not one of them harmed. It was too bad, but enough to frighten us all away but Good. The loss was too great for the Irishman; he could not give up "his goose for to-morrow," and instead of running off up the road with us, he gathered his stick, and singling out his gander went for him. Up by the barn-yard gate they went, now across the road, now down the lane by the house, Good's diminutive pot legs plying vigorously, and the old gander flapping and flapping, and making the very night silence shake with his "quack! quack! quack!" Just as the enthusiastic young man was about to make his levy near the yard-gate, suddenly, like a peal of thunder, a pack of hounds broke from a kennel upon him. We heard the attack several hundred yards up the road, and stopped for the result. The wonder is that they did not tear him all to pieces, for he took the right course to that end. Hardly had we turned about till we saw the frightened

Irishman come flying up the road (I mean in his way) with a dozen hounds at his heels, snapping and barking, and he piteously calling, in a subdued voice, "boys, boys;" with a blanket in one hand and his cane in the other, striking furiously to the right and to the left. As momentous as was the occasion, sobriety had more than it could bear. We were all convulsed with laughter:

"Drive off the d——d dogs," he cried, as he ran into our midst, almost out of breath; "you'd laugh to see a man tore to pieces, wouldn't you?"

The dogs were as cowardly as Good, for soon as we showed fight with our sticks, they retreated rapidly. We called Good "goosey" afterwards.

Meat was plenty enough after we learned how it was to be had. South Carolina, poor as it is for agricultural purposes, supplies a good many pigs, and they were fat and fine in the fall of 1864. A family of darling little porkers, weighing fifteen or twenty pounds each, might have been found almost any night, asleep with their mother, in a fence corner or pen. It was a trifling matter to slip up and seize one of the little sleepers by the hind legs and dash his brains out against the ground before he had time to squeal, else to take a heavy stick and knock him to his eternal sleep without awaking him from his temporal. Then it was easy to bleed him with a pocket knife, and just as easy to throw him on the shoulder and carry him to the woods, skin, and cut out of his tender flesh whatever was convenient to carry, and leave the carcass to the crows. Of course we did not kill any of them in this way, for it was against the law, but if we happened to have any fresh pork or sweet potatoes to cook we had no trouble in accomplishing it. Before going under the leaves for the day, and as soon as it got light enough to see, we would provide a couple of stones, three inches in diameter, a tin cup of water, and quite a bundle of dry faggots, the size of a rye straw, from the bushes round about. With these at our heads we could go to sleep. During the day, when any one waked up and wanted something to eat, something warm and good, he would turn over on his face, set the Savannah tin pan upon the two stones, place some dry faggots underneath, strike a match, set them on fire, put in his meat, well salted and *washed*; keep adding as his faggots burned out, and in half the time he could get it at home, he was eating his meat and potatoes, his corn bread and gravy, with epicurean pleasure. This tin pan was as valuable as the magician's wand. We would fry meat, boil potatoes and make coffee in it, all the same hour.

One night, a few miles northeast of Greenville, S. C., we took tea, by invitation with a party of colored folks, one Martin, a "yaller man," of Pogram extraction being the principal deacon of the occasion. The feast was pre-arranged by fourteen hours, and Martin spared no efforts or liberality to make it a feast of fat things. Moses, Martin's oldest son, had enough of the predominant Pogram in him to make him second in rank in the service, and it was he that led us from the cane-brake to the reception under the hill.

After the usual salutations, we surrounded the table, or, rather the table cloth, spread upon the ground. There was upon it four white plates, four cups and saucers, knives, forks, &c. To eat, there was in the center a nicely dressed hen at one end, a cord of ginger bread at the other, a pot full of steaming coffee, with pumpkin pies and other things intervening; and everything was well prepared and good. Yes, actually good, any place; and from their chuckling and askance looks as we munched their provender, I am certain that we left our host with a good opinion of Yankee capacity for food.

Martin was determined that Moses should join our party.

"He is de sharpest boy in all de country; every body says so; and I want him to go to de Noff to git larnin."

Without consulting us as to our pleasure in the matter, he went all over the country that day, offering sixty dollars for a pair of shoes to fix off Moses; but he failed to get them, and we persuaded the anxious paternal that his hopeful could not possibly make the trip without them.

Our eyes were as heavy as our haversacks that night when we went upon the road. Good was in front, and suffered his mind to recur too much to the little episodes of the evening, perhaps, for he let two horsemen ride up within a hundred yards of our front before he "hissed." To the left was a field, to the right an open forest, without bushes or weeds, but appearing best for our escape, Good took it in a twinkle, and we after him. Twenty yards from the roadside we fell upon our faces, with heads to heels, to form the appearance of a log, and lay as still. I think the moon was shining, for it was almost light enough to count the buttons upon the strangers' coats.

Chisman's heel struck me in the forhead, when we heard the rattling of sabres. They were two cavalrymen, and had seen us, too. Just opposite where we laid, nearly breathless, they reined up their horses and stood gazing in our direction.

"Sam, I'll be —— if I didn't see a man."

"Are you sure?"

"Yes, I'm sure."

"Oh, I guess it might have been a cow."

"No, sir; I'll be —— if it wasn't a *man*."

"Well, if it was a man, where do you think he is by this time?"

"I don't know, but it was a man, sure."

"Well, it was somebody's nigger, if you did see one; 'les go on."

We always thought they were afraid, or they would have ridden a little way into the woods; but when they rode on without it they had our full approbation. Good laid for nearly a half hour after they left, before he could find heart enough to "hiss" back upon the road. This was another stimulus to caution.

We longed much for the loyal white men of North Carolina, whom we had heard so much about all along the way, and we were now very near their border. We felt that as soon as we placed South Carolina at our backs, that our work would be almost done—that we would be nearly home. The night that we expected to pass the border, we walked with perhaps more spirit than on any other occasion. Right on we pushed, through branches, over hills, up the side of the Blue Ridge, till about midnight, when we came upon a pillar of hewn limestone, standing six feet out of the ground, upon the summit of a mountain, on the south face of which was inscribed "S. C., 1819," and on the north face, "N. C., 1849."

Eureka and amen! We had at last reached the much desired point which marked the division between friends and foes. So we did not tarry long, but shaking the South Carolina dust from our feet, we spat once more upon the hated State and went on. We skipped down the side of the mountain into North Carolina, with heels and hearts as light as homeward bound school boys. But had it been possible, and had we but lifted the curtain that hid from us the next twenty days and saw the loads of trouble and hardships that awaited us, we would have been almost persuaded to turn back to prison, for while we felt that we were almost home, and the difficulties almost overcome, the facts were that we had hardly passed through the preliminaries to the great system of troubles that awaited us.

In the first place, the first night after entering the State we had trouble among ourselves. We happened upon a negro man who was going to start next morning for Ashville, sixty miles, with two bales of stocking yarn for the rebel government. He was going to drive four mules, fill up his wagon with stripped corn blades; and his master had a brother living four miles north of Ashville. This fellow entreated us to join him; he would cover us up in his wagon with the fodder, haul us to Ashville in two days, take us through town to his master's brother on the other side, get there in the night, unhitch his four mules and give them to us, and he would steal one from his master's brother, and with the mules we could ride to the Yankees, thirty miles beyond, the same night. Two wanted to join the negro, and two did not. Chisman and I thought that since we had come so far successfully, we would not assume any unnecessary hazards to save a little labor and time. Baker and Good thought it a rare chance. We all had confidence enough in the negro, but there were these difficulties apprehended by Chisman and myself: There were two thousand troops at Ashville, and foraging parties daily putting out on all the roads for many miles. One of these parties might seize the fodder of the negro and find us underneath it, or they might search the wagon for contraband goods; or some one might get into the wagon along the road to ride, and take position on us. These were our principal reasons for objection; but besides, we had a mind to doubt that the Yankees were only thirty miles from Ashville. Then we also feared that if we were captured in company with a negro, that it would be an excuse for the rebels to hand us over to the civil authorities, to be dealt with as kidnappers, instead of prisoners of war. This last reason led to a spirited dispute, which, I am ashamed to say, culminated in blows, the character and extent of which, the public would blame me if I told. Here we came near having a rupture—a division of the party—but under the arbirtary circumstances alone, the matter was dismissed, or suspended, and we journeyed on as before, leaving the negro behind.

The next night began a chapter of troubles. We came to a respectable looking farm house sitting very near the roadside. Houses of this class we had generally gone round, but since we were now in North Carolina, in the land of the loyal, and after listening a few minutes the leader decided to move on past the house independently. It was four o'clock in the morning, and nothing seemed to be astir or awake, as we moved up silently in the bright moonlight; but, when just opposite the door, and when least expected, a pack of hounds broke from under the porch upon us in an instant. They were too soon upon us, and too numerous to then think of flying, so we hastily "rallied by fours," to use a military term, or placed our backs together, thus facing in all directions, and began a vigorous battle with our clubs. While thus engaged, the gentleman (?) of the house opened and stood in the door, in his night clothes, within thirty feet of us, afraid to speak or retire. We could less stand his eyes than the dogs, and we broke up our position of defense and ran off up the road, striking as we went.

Having reached the woods on the other side of the house, and driven off the dogs, we stopped for a moment under a tree to consult. That we had been seen by a white man this time, was certain, and that he had a pack of fierce hounds was also certain. Besides, it was nearly morning, and at daylight our tracks could be easily recognized and scented. Again, what must we do? Everybody will say as we did: "Why, leave the road and get just as far away from there before day as possible, and in as puzzling a manner as possible."

Into the woods we went, through branches and up branches, now walking backwards, now forwards; now walking on the fences with long poles, turning the top rails over as we passed, now stepping in each other's tracks and dragging a wet blanket after us, all the time doing our very best for distance—sometimes by the roadside, sometimes in the field. I never labored so hard in my life for an hour and a half, and I think we must have walked and ran at least six miles in the time; and we might have gone even farther had we not come to a cross roads, with a few unimportant houses about; maybe a blacksmith and a grog shop, all possessed by the lord of that rich looking mansion two hundred yards to the left, with a long row of negro huts stretched in the background. It was these negro huts that induced us to stop as soon as we did, for they had become distressingly scarce along the road; so much so, that for the last two nights we had been bothered in getting enough to eat; and, as we expected soon to enter the mountains proper, this was perhaps the last opportunity we would have to get aid from the negroes; and some how or other the "good Union people" we had heard so much about were always a little ahead.

We went into concealment as convenient to the huts as possible. And that was another day of extraordinary suspense and anxiety. Every dog that barked to the south of us was hounds following the trail; every squirrel that jumped in the leaves was a man's footfall. Nobody had anything to eat but shelled corn, yet, nobody got hungry that day; none of us had slept a moment the night before, but nobody's eyes were closed or ears stopped for the twelve long hours we lay in the chestnut tree-top. If one would turn over or stretch out his legs, or draw them up so as to rattle the leaves, his three companions would in concert whisper: "Be still. Don't make so much noise." Although concealed in the midst of a forest, in an excellent place, and perhaps not a human being within a quarter of a mile all day, yet all this caution seemed necessary, for those two eyes that looked at us from the door the morning before followed, haunted, and stared at us all the time. They were in our eye-lids, they were under the blanket, they were in the azure space— everywhere, like demons around the demented inebriate. But when night came, we still lay under our leaves, unmolested by either dogs or rebels.

About 10 o'clock Leader with No. 2 started for the huts, dodging through the corn, as but few times before. This expedition came near being abandoned after all, on account of our fright the morning before; but fearing we could find nothing at all to eat in the mountains we entered upon it as our last chance. A negro man was found without much effort, and led out into the field for a consultation. For ten minutes after the party all joined him he was frightened nearly to death.

"Lawdy! Ef you all is Yankees you bettah be gittin' away from here, for Massa Cap'n Pace's got his comp'ny out dis night to cotch Yankees. He says Massa Ross seed some pass his house dis monin' 'foh day, and dey's somewha in dis country yit. But if you all is Yankees you won't hurt no cullud people, will you? I doesn't go about much, but brudder Reuben he knows a heap; ev'rybody says Ruben is sharp, an Reuben he say de Yankees am good people."

"And where is Reuben?"

"Lod bress you! he's on guard, wid a gun, watchin' at de Cross Roads for Yankees."

"Who put him there?"

"Massa Pace; and I got to take his place in half an hour.

"We conversed with the fellow several minutes, and

though apparently willing we were not satisfied to trust him with the superintendence of anything, he was so ignorant and unfamiliar with everything, and though very hungry we preferred that Reuben, that sharp colored man, should look after something for us to eat.

This fellow said he would go and tell Reuben about us being down in the field, and he knew that Reuben would come to us, "for he do want to see de Yankees de wust."

We dismissed him after exacting from him a promise to break his secret to none but Reuben, and told him to send Reuben to us at the water gap. A little doubtful of Reuben's admiration of Northerners, from the fact that he was standing guard to catch them, we withdrew fifty yards from the water gap and laid down under some bushes to watch.

I am sorry that the katydid was so relentless in her song that night, for as much as I used to admire this pleasant little serenader, when she sings at my window now she disturbs my sleep.

The day had been one of extraordinary suspense in consequence of having been seen the morning before, and night had brought to us the confirmation of our fears that the country was all astir over the appearance of a gang of men supposed to be Federal soldiers. And would it be prudent, or even rational, for us to lay within gun-shot of a rebel company and wait for a negro to stack his gun and visit us, the very objects of their alarm, as a friend? Then, if ever so desirous of helping us, how could he be in the very presence of the rebels with any safety to himself or us, when the rebels were likely to call him at any moment for duty? But before us frowned the in-hospitable mountains, within two hours' walk, and how could we think of entering them, more than a hundred miles across, the last of November, with scarce a pint of shelled corn to the man? Then, if we attempted to march that night without more reliable information than we had received, what moment would we not expect to be fired on or halted by some lurking lookout?

Under these discouraging circumstances we smoked and waited for the coming of Reuben, while the sharp shrill notes of numberless katydids were poured forth unceasingly, like the whippo-wils of the Rapidan, adding ten fold to our loneliness and fear. But—

"Listen!" said Baker. "I hear somebody tramping through the stubble. It may be Reuben."

"Yes; I hear it plain," responded all three; and soon the form of a monstrous looking individual was seen slipping across the wheat field. Straight to the water gap he went and whistled a few times gently.

Satisfied that it must be Reuben we went to him. Sure enough, it was the sharp colored man who had been on guard, and a very different man from the one who had been there before. Reuben was forty years old, he said, and a laugh-and-grow-fat sort of man, round, and as vain as a titled Englishman; a regular Count Fusco, all the time in a silly laugh. In a perfect convulsion of laughter he seized our hands, two at a time, and gave them each a regular lover's squeeze, holding on and crushing away for a minute or two.

"What is the matter with you?" inquired Chisman a little piqued.

"Why, you see, ole massa—ha, ha, ha, ha—ole massa—ha, ha, ha, ha—has me tryin' to catch you gemmin, for two hours—ha, ha, ha, ha——"

"Well hush up, you fool you. Quit your laughing and tell us all about it," replied Chisman, rather unevangelically.

"What! Catch you Yankees! Why, sah, I'd radder ctach my granmudder runnin' from de debil—ha, ha, ha."

"But, sir, we do beg of you to hush laughing so, for

some one may hear you and it may lead to our capture."

"What! Yoa capture. Why one of you gemmen might take a big rock and run ebry man home Massa Cap'n Pace's got, and me too, if I was on guard like I was. Ha, ha, ha."

"But come, uncle; I say quit laughing and tell us what about Captain Pace and what they are doing up at the house, or we will swallow you alive."

"Tink you'll have a heavy stomach if you swallow me, sah. Ha, ha, ha."

We got altogether out of patience with Reuben before we got the laughter out of him sufficiently to talk intelligibly. Then he proceeded in his way to tell us as his brother had in part how Massa Ross had seen four men pass his house a little before daylight that morning, whom he took for Yankees. Captain Pace had been notified of this fact and had called out his company of men to watch for us that night, and had been assured by Ross that the strangers could not possibly have passed the Cross Roads, up by "my Massa," before light, and it was along the road from the Cross to Ross' that twenty men were posted, with guns to watch for somebody, evidently us.

The war having called every able-bodied male between sixteen and sixty into the army, the remaining old men and little boys over the country were organized into emergency companies, and armed to repel raids, to suppress insurrections, and for such other emergencies as might arise.

Pace was the captain of one of these companies, and his actions on this occasion, perhaps his first official duty, were much better described by Reuben than they will be by me. He said the King's officer was mounted on an old white horse, galloping from post to post, armed with a sabre, two revolvers and a shot gun—and Reuben said once that he had a piece of artillery mounted behind him, but he took that back.

To be sure of adequate force for four disarmed Yankees the gallant captain had called three or four trusty negroes to supply the place of absentees. Two or three times the brave captain rode up to him with:

"Now, Reuben, remember to halt them three times, and if they don't then stop, fire at 'em and aim low. Look carefully and be still, and if we don't catch the rascals to-night, why, call me a coward."

Reuben was just the man for us to see, for he had intelligence enough to advise and humor enough to cheer us. In spite of our first impulses and our surroundings the fellow would provoke from us an occasional laugh—not that his tale was so funny, but that his humor and expression were.

His story about running off to the Yankees was rich. His master sent him on an errand to Hendersonville and while there a notion came into his head to go to the Federals, and away he went for the Tennessee line.

Our forces were at Bull Gap, and reaching a mountain that overlooked their camp fires his heart failed him and he lay there watching the smoke and light for two days and nights, eating nothing but huckleberries. This growing dull he retraced his steps homeward, fully convinced in his own mind that the Yankees were a bad people and would have killed him instantly if he had gone to them. When he reached home he told his master that while at Hendersonville a rebel officer found him and made him go to Ashville and work on the fortifications.

Reuben's first advice was not to think at all of trying to travel any that night. He did not know how far the report had spread about there being Yankees in the country, and the rebels might be on the lookout for us at some other point, for people were likely to be unusually watchful to-night, anyhow, and he wanted to talk with us a "long time," and he knew where to hide us for the next day, that would puzzle our shadows to find us. We decided to tarry as advised. Then the next thing was something to eat. We had been nearly thirty hours on nothing but shelled corn, and now that we had agreed to lay over a day, and to be so securely hid, we began to feel some emotions about something more substantial to eat than corn. Upon this point we sobered Reuben effectually, for we treated of a fact that vitally interested him.

"Can you give us something to eat, Reuben?—we're mighty hungry."

"Oh, yes, sah! oh, yes, sah!—git you something to eat, sho; but, gemmen, massa mighty hard on us; doesn't gib us hardly nuffin to eat; but, gemmen, you shill have plenty to eat, if I has to steal for you—and, golly, I'se good at dat."

Now, Reuben remembering that he had been with us an hour, and that they might miss him up at the Cross Roads, and involve him in suspicious circumstances, he hurried us off to a spur of the mountain, and to a large shelving rock, covered with a chestnut tree-top, a place familiar with other darkies of the plantation, and leaving us here, he said that if he could not come again soon with something to eat, he would send another colored person.

Reuben, chuckling over the good joke of standing guard for us and hiding us, all in the same hour, started in a bear gallop down the declivity to his post of duty, and we had nothing further from him until after midnight, when he came leading the way up to our concealment, followed by his ignorant brother, Jubal, and two wenches, bearing a big pot of boiled cabbage. The boys had both been discharged from further duty as guards.

"Golly, gemmen, we's got you's a pot of mighty good cabbage—we wus gwine to hab it for dinner to-morrow, but my wife said she'd cook it for youens."

There was the cabbage, submerged in the liquor, and still warm and delicious. Too hungry to empty it in our tin pan, or to make wooden forks to lift it out—too hungry to wait a moment for polite preparation—into the liquor we went with thumbs and fingers for a bite, and they went in and out with astonishing rapidity. If I could hope to sustain the statement, I would deny that I was as greedy as the rest, tor they will all be ashamed when I tell the public how they, jealous of each other's share, increased their feeding capacity from a thumb and one finger, to a thumb and two fingers, and before the pot was emptied, the whole hand was on duty; then they scuffled and pushed over the liquor, like hungry swine over a swill bucket. I never heard any of my company testify upon this point, but it is the present opinion of the writer that he demeaned himself on the occasion with distinguished reservation. This much I am clear on, that Chisman, being the lion of the party, took two drinks to the other's one, which usurpation stands to his debit to this day. And I also remember poor little three hundred pounds Reuben, as he stood near by, "dumb as a lamb before his shearers," to see such a rapacious onset upon his pot of cabbage. He felt such assurance that it would be sufficient for our suppers, that when he saw it so hastily disappear, he was troubled about having nothing more to give us. But he did nothing more that night than promise that the next day we should have plenty of sweet potatoes and bread. A short time before daylight he and his party left us, and went back to their huts.

All the following day we lay under the rock where Reuben put us, and got nothing more to eat till four o'clock in the afternoon, when Jubal brought a considerable quantity of roasted potatoes in his shirt bosom. At dark Reuben came again and brought us a little bread, saying "it was the last spoonful of meal he could find among the colored folks," and that they would draw no more until to-morrow afternoon. The food was dispatched almost as soon as brought; and even then, when we started that night to penetrate the mountains, before morning we were very hungry, and not a morsel in our haversacks but a few grains of parched corn.

Captain Pace lived on the road yet before us, half a mile, and Reuben thought it judicious not to pass along the road by his house. We were disposed to act upon his suggestion, and shook farewell with our jolly friend, with the intention to not disturb the gallant warrior, resting from his labors of the night before, if possible. So we pulled off around the spur of the mountain until blockaded by ledges and laurels, then we went down in the valley near the road and tried it, but the briars and bushes confronting us there put into our minds a notion to take the road at all hazards by the gentleman's house.

The Captain's house was close at hand when we stepped into the road, after ten o'clock.

If any reader should ever travel the highway leading from Hendersonville, N. C., to Greenville, S. C., and should be on the lookout when eight miles from Saluda Gap, he will see on the east side, fifty yards from the road, an old one-story frame house, quietly going to decay, with a porch the full length of the front, and two or three log buildings on the flank; and this place he may write down as the residence of the chivalrous Pace. Then it may be of interest to stop when a half mile farther south, and look to the west through a narrow strip of shrubby timber into a field, skirted on the north by a branch and a range of hillocks, covered by dwarfish oak and chestnut, and contemplate that it was near the north-east corner of that field we held our first converse with the facetious Reuben.

We stopped at that point several minutes to listen, but seeing no light and hearing no noise, we started on tiptoe to pass. We all chuckled considerably as we cleared the house and stable without disturbing even the dog, and leader was beginning to set his feet down with assurance, when suddenly he recoiled, even back to No. 2, at the appearance of a white man in his front not twenty feet away.

So suddenly did this undesirable meeting come upon the leader, that he had neither time nor power to signal or make a flight. Meeting a white man face to face upon a public highway, within two hundred yards of an officer's residence, was an event not prepared for, and there was no genius in the company to extricate us from the difficulty. The halting in front without signal caused the intervals to be closed up in an instant; and there we stood, for something better to do, breast to back, stiff and straight as four statues. The man was evidently as much scared as we were, for, after halting a moment in the road, he began to shy around us, and shied even as far as the fence would let him; and when directly opposite our flank, and while stepping sideways, ten feet at a time, he stammered out spasmodically—

"W-h-o, w-h-o a-r-e y-o-u's?"

The leader, slowly stretching forth his hand and stick, like a spectre, replied in a ghostly, guttural tone—

"M-o-v-e o-n."

The man picked himself up like a steel trap, and I never saw such vigorous running but once before in my life, and that was by Good and the hounds. Slam went Pace's gate, bang went his door, and we never heard anything more of this stranger. It might not have been the veritable Captain, but from the manner he entered the gate and house, he must have been quite familiar with the premises. And if it was, this circumstance should not be taken to redound discredit upon that gentleman's valor, for verily, in those troubled times, to meet, at the hour of midnight, four men who act so strangely, is inclined to "harrow up the soul" of the bravest.

Reuben had prepared us for considerable adventure that night, but for only a small portion of what was in store. Eight miles ahead was the Saluda Gap, which, if we found guarded, as was expected, we must not attempt to pass. Thirteen miles ahead was Flat Rock, a famous watering place before the war, but at this time the hotel and hospital were converted into storehouses for valuables, and guarded by a company of soldiers.

After thirty-six hours rest with Reuben, and adventure with Pace, we hurried on with good speed, and two hours and a half brought us beneath the frowning hights of the Saluda Mountains. The river of the same name, at this point, being near its source, was small, but went dashing and splashing along its rocky bed, more noisy than the Ganges. We found a bridge across the river, which Reuben had told us was not guarded, and having full confidence in the statement we ventured on and over it after a slight reconnoisance. But the worst had not yet come. At one point the road and river squeezed themselves, side by side, through the narrow defile in the mountains, and it was here that we expected trouble. This being about the only passable place through the mountains for many miles, a guard had been maintained here for several months, to catch refugees and deserters from the rebel army. Reuben had said that if we found this pass guarded an attempt to go through would be capture, and an attempt to go over the mountain to the right or to the left, would be fraught with much peril and hardship; that the mountains were very steep and very rough and dangerous to a stranger in the night-time.

"Hist!" said leader, "isn't that a light in the road?"

"It is," whispered number two.

"Well, then, it is the guard, and what shall we do?" Mountains are dismal things in the night. The mountaineer himself shuns them after the sun goes down.

There they were before us, apparently half-way to Heaven, and forming what seemed to us at that moment an insurmountable wall between hope and home. We stood between the river and the road when we discovered the light. The road, after crossing the river, put off five or six hundred yards to meet another highway that came there to get through the mountains, then curved around to the pass and light alluded to. At the junction of the roads was somebody's store and blacksmith shop, besides a few residences.

To go over the mountains, we must do one of two things. We must either go and recross the river at the bridge, and take our chances in getting over it at some other point, or we must go around the village and over the mountains to the left. As both these difficulties seemed fully equal to running the guard in the pass, the leader decided that we would reconnoiter the latter, at least before choosing either of the former.

Clinging to the river, we glided like a mist up the bank, squatting at every roll of a pebble or crack of a weed. We approached within a hundred yards of the guard, rested on our knees, watched, listened, whispered. The soldier had a little fire built against the side of the mountain, and was sitting very still with his back to the river. Leader crawled up still closer, returned and reported that in his opinion the guard was asleep—that he was sitting with his head resting upon his hands, his gun lying across his lap, and in this position he saw him ten minutes without stirring—thought, with great caution, we might slip by him. At it we went, sliding and dragging along, feeling every inch of the way for loose stones or dry weeds, breathing as noiselessly as the rocks, eyes all the time fixed upon the man that might, at one time, have stretched himself up and driven us through with his bayonet. Twenty feet from his back, and still he sleeps. Ten feet past him, and still he sleeps; fifty feet past him, and he awakes not. Up! up on our feet, and we bound along that road like frightened deer for the next half mile.

Safe from the principal danger, thought we, as we pushed on to Flat Rock, five miles distant. The moon came up soon after midnight, and when we got into the neighborhood of Flat Rock, it was well up into the heavens and breaking out ever and anon through the hurrying clouds. The spacious hotel and hospital in the midst of a park, we saw long before we reached it, and even before we saw the fire of the pickets, a considerable distance below, upon the appearance of which we went into the woods, designing to make a semi-circle of a mile and a half, as we had been told by Reuben that would be sufficient to avoid all the pickets. At one point in the semi-circle we crossed a country road, and immediately upon passing into the woods on the other side, the two rear men, Chisman and Good, came running upon us in front, averring that we had nearly run over a picket, who turned and spit as they passed him in the edge of the woods. Chisman avers to this day that he could have knocked him down with his stick if he had had a mind to do it. We all agreed that the fellow must be a consummate coward, or he would have said something as we passed. Perhaps we turned back into the road before we had gone the mile and a half as directed, although we did not think so then; but our anxiety to reach the neighborhood of Hendersonville that night, where Reuben had said we would find some negroes and food, might have misled our judgment. At all events we entered the road too soon.

Ahead of us a short distance we at once perceived in the moonlight an old dilapidated building of some sort, setting by the road side. We stopped and listened several minutes, as was our custom, but upon hearing and seeing nothing we went along unsuspiciously in our regular order. By the light of the moon an object might be seen a considerable distance, and there were eyes upon us much nearer than we thought. The old building sat with its end to the road, and just as Leader came up with it—I tremble now as I tell it—out stepped four men at our very side. The moment our eyes fell upon them we saw that one had a sword at his side, and the other three had cartridge boxes on. Of course we all stopped mechanically, for the surprise had petrified us. The man with the sword on, spoke:

"Good morning, gentlemen."

Leader responded—"Good morning, sir."

"Are you traveling?"

"Yes, sir."

"Where are you going?"

"Going home, sir."

"Where do you live?"

"Up in the north part of Henderson county?"

"You are soldiers, I suppose?"

"Yes, sir."

"What regiment do you belong to?"

"Eighteenth North Carolina, sir."

"Where is your regiment now?"

"It's at Charleston."

"Who's your Colonel now—I believe I don't know?"

"James Dawson."

" Were you all in the fight at John's Island the other day?"

"Yes, sir?"

"Oh, yes, I believe your Colonel was wounded there—wasn't he?"

"Well, I don't know whether you would consider him wounded or not; his horse was killed and fell on him and bruised him badly, so that he has not been on duty since."

The truth was we knew as much about the Eighteenth North Carolina as he did, and from our prompt answers to his questions he had a mind to pass us by, but just at that moment the moon glided out from under a cloud and betrayed us with her light, by showing Yankee clothes on two of the party.

The officer, seeing the suspicious uniform, stepped up with "What are you doing with them blue clothes on? You are all d—d Yankees, and may consider yourselves my prisoners," at the same time drawing his sword from its scabbard.

I was resigned, so was Chisman and Baker, and everybody else would have been under the circumstances, but Good. He was the right man in the right place. Little did we think, as his short legs vexed us in the streets of Laurensville, or as we had often unkindly laughed at him about the gander, that he was yet to be the "Moses to lead us out of bondage." He stood behind, dumb as the rocks, until he saw that he was going to be surrendered, then he spoke up:

"Not yet, Captain."

Whereupon the Captain turned and flew at him with uplifted blade, and I was sure was going to split him from head to foot; but Good, undaunted, deliberately raised his stick to the position of guard, and not moving out of his tracks, continued:

"Hold on, Captain, hold on!—you surely will not strike an unarmed boy?"

The coolness of the Irishman nonplussed the Captain, and he turned upon his men, who were standing by with eyes and mouths wide open, and roared:

"Why don't you get your guns and arrest these men, and not stand here like brutes?"

Immediately the men broke into the house for their guns, and Good, turning about, broke back the road like a wild horse with parted rein.

We all followed from instinct, if from no other cause, and the Captain after us in full speed, flourishing his blade and screaming every jump, "Halt! halt! halt!" But we did not halt. Over fences and fields; over logs and ledges, over briars and bushes, we flew, waiting not to listen for our pursuers. We had heard the negroes say that when the rebels got after the Union men they always run to the mountains; and we, not knowing what better to do, broke for one also. It was an isolated mountain, having no connection whatever with the general range standing off among the hills as a vidette to the main chain, two miles behind it, and it was two miles away to the southwest, but we ran to it without a single stop, and up its rugged side, climbing over rocks, crawling through laurel bushes, till the very summit was reached, before we sat down to rest.

It was now after three o'clock in the morning. The wind had raised to quite a gale, and the clouds were thickening up fast. We found the mountain so rough as to make it quite dangerous to travel, so we decided to wait till daylight before resuming our journey or trying to get off that mountain; and this latter was very desirable, inasmuch as we feared the rebels might suspect we were on it, and come to hunt for us with dogs the following day.

When light came, the rain was pouring down in torrents. Innumerable woody hills were spread out before us on every side, but no way to reach any of them without crossing open fields, and there were houses thick around us. To stay upon the mountain and probably be hunted with men and dogs, seemed too great a risk, but to pass away over the open plain, studded with houses, seemed to be a greater.

Our dilemma was so confounding that we did not decide upon anything, but kept lingering and lingering, in a stupor, upon that bleak summit. It was a time when the stoutest heart must surrender. The elements seemed to be our enemies too. By ten o'clock we were as wet as if we had been standing in a river, and the atmosphere rapidly changing to cold. At eleven o'clock it was sleeting—at twelve o'clock snowing.

O, Heaven! what have we done that you will spread out, over the face of the earth, in the very midst of our enemies, a certain snare to our feet. Could it be possible that such a snow was going to fall as would make our further progress impossible, on account of our tracks, and yet it was coming down rapidly. This day culminated our trouble, and it seemed that one feather more would have broken the camel's back. Hungry, wet, cold, driven from our course to an unknown mountain by our enemies; lost, and without a friend or guide, or a compass or map. We were in great distress, having been hungry for three days, and nothing at all to eat since the evening before, but a few grains of corn, and they were all gone long before noon, and with empty haversacks and heavy hearts, stood on a clift of rocks, shaking away, hours at a time, without speaking a word. The difficulties that now arose about us, seemed altogether insurmountable. We must have food, we must have warmth, we must have information, and yet it seemed that we could have nothing but capture or death. To have gone from our hiding place into South Carolina, and given ourselves up, would have been a great task, but our impassionate desire to escape, fed as we approached North by the hope of success, made the task in Western North Carolina too much to bear. Sitting by a cheerful fire, in a circle of friends, in the midst of comfort and competency, and in a time of peace, this may seem but a trifling occasion, for it is hard under such circumstances to conceive, even approximately, the vast extreme of human endurance and human distress. There are no words in the language that can convey a correct idea of our anguish of mind and real suffering of body, on this Sunday, on that North Carolina mountain.

It did not snow long nor much, but it grew very cold—so cold that the snow became so light and frozen that it was blown like chaff into the valley below. The wind blew from the northwest in tornadoes, and drove the frost from that side of the mountain in clouds, in our faces and against our backs.

At two o'clock in the afternoon we found a shelving rock and crawled under it for shelter, and under it we got colder than before, but we lay there an hour, and until the fear of a freezing stupor drove us out. One of the party having nothing on his body but a thin blouse and an old pair of pants, begged for a fire to keep him from freezing, but the others, a little better provided, refused him by force. Then we selected a big rock, well covered from the valley, on the leeward side of the mountain, and ran around it rapidly until the blood ran warmer in our veins.

During the day we noticed on the south side of the mountain, near its base, a cove, in which was a cleared off spot of an acre or more. From the mountain top we could see that this spot was cultivated, and that it had on it at the time some sort of vegetation that looked like turnips. All day long we watched it as anxiously as if there had been danger of its slipping away. If the production were turnips, then at nightfall what pleasure we would have in munching our fill of that delicious vegetable, and such loads as we would carry with us would be amazing. These thoughts occupied much of our minds in the afternoon, and so much that by four o'clock we were half frenzied about something to eat, and it appeared that turnips were the very things we wanted most.

Having seen no demonstrations about the mountain during the day that indicated search, at 4 o'clock we could no longer resist the temptation of descending for a few of those turnips, at least. Arriving within a hundred yards of the patch, we discovered that the crop was cabbage, instead of turnips; and disappointment brooded over us again. But cabbage was better than nothing, and some of them we must have. So, three of us took shelter in a cluster of laurel bushes near by, while the Irishman sallied forth for the forage.

He crawled along to the fence, slipped through a crack, into the patch, and succeeded in breaking the only knife blade of the party in the first cabbage stock. The ground was so frozen that he could not pull them out, and after two or three ineffectual efforts at pulling them out or breaking them off, he set about the twisting process.

By this mode he had succeeded in getting four or five heads ready for exportation, and was industriously engaged wringing another, when suddenly somebody shouted at him from the other side:

"Oh, you rogue! I always thought you would steal; and now I know it, for we've caught you in the very act."

Good sprang upright, whirled around, gazed, and there to his great confusion stood four grown ladies, on the opposite side of the fence, looking directly at him. He abandoned his enterprise in a hurry and came tearing up to the laurel with a single cabbage in his hand, the women continuing the while:

"Yes, I would run, now I was caught—you had better run and beg our mercy, you rascal you," laughing heartily all the time.

Good having crouched with us in the bushes, the women held a short conversation, and then started straight for us. And now was a greater dilemma than ever. If we ran, we would have to climb the mountain in their sight, and thus expose the four of us; and if we staid there we were sure to come face to face with white faces, in daylight. We decided, however, they could do no more than tell on us, and they could do that in either case. Four unarmed women, we thought, can not capture us by force, and when they leave us we can run away and hide. So we all sat side by side, on an old log, to abide the consequences.

Nearer and nearer they approached, pushing their way through the bushes, laughing and giggling as they came.

Desperate and disconsolate we sat, like four blind owls, perched on our log, moving neither head nor foot. On they came, in their glee, peeping and prying, till they stepped into an avenue, a few feet away, and looked squarely at us. Then they quickly turned and began a hasty retreat. They evidently expected to see some acquaintance, but instead thereof saw four as strange, haggard, ugly, repulsive looking men as could well be imagined. Subsequent events proved that they took Good for one of the neighbor boys who was hiding out in the mountains to keep out of the rebel army.

Desiring to allay their fear, if possible, we called after them.

"Halloo! girls; don't be scared—we are probably more your friends than you think."

They answered, "Who are you?"

"We are soldiers."

"What kind of soldiers?"

"Confederate soldiers, of course."

"Yes fighting for that miserable old scamp of a Jeff. Davis, are you? You ought to be ashamed of yourselves."

"Why ought we to be ashamed?"

"There is why enough. The old rascal fetched this on the country. The Yankees didn't want war at all."

"Well, if the Yankees didn't want war, what made them come down here to invade our homes and steal our niggers?"

"Why, they just came down to whip you rebels—that's all they came for—and they are going to do it, too."

"Why, do you think we should be so cowardly as to stay at home and see the Yankees overrun our country, burn our houses, steal our horses and negroes, insult our women, and such like, without taking up arms against them?"

"They ain't doing any such thing; they aint running over the country half fast enough, or burning half houses enough to suit me. I'd like to see the Yankees coming this very minute, I'd risk their burning our house, and stealing our horses and negroes."

"Can it be possible that such beautiful girls as you, in old North Carolina, are in sympathy with the Yankees?"

"It can be possible that such ugly girls as we, in old North Carolina, are not in sympathy with the hateful rebels who hide around to kill our brothers because they won't fight for them."

A ray of hope flashed upon us. We were now in that country where Union people were said to abound, and these girls, notwithstanding our many efforts to draw from them expressions to the contrary, so boldly asserting their full sympathy with the Federal arms, gave us assurance enough to break to them our secret.

"You say you like the Yankees?"

"Yes."

"And would like to see them?"

"Yes."

"Well, then," said one of us, "look here, upon this log—look at us from head to foot, and you will see four live and as full-blooded Yankees as are found anywhere. We are four Yankee prisoners, who have escaped from the rebels at Columbia, and are trying to make our way to the Federal lines at Knoxville. We are now lost, nearly frozen and nearly starved, and if you are the friend to Yankees you appear to be, we humbly beg to become the objects of your charity."

"Law, Juan," said Florence, the youngest, a sweet, modest maiden of sixteen summers, "I'll bet these are the same men that Captain Henry was telling us about to-day at dinner. Did you all talk with anybody last night at Flat Rock?"

"We talked with some men, over on the road some place."

"And been on this mountain all the time since?"

"Yes."

"Why they think you are here, and there have been men hunting and watching for you all day, and the Captain eat dinner at our house to-day."

By this time they had returned to the bushes, even to the log upon which we sat, and extended to us their hands of friendship and fidelity. The greeting they gave us was enough, for there is a language in the shaking of hands that carries with it more meaning, and less deceit than any articulate sounds. If the heart is warm, and full of kind and generous feeling which it wishes to reciprocate, it will generally tell you so by the earnest manner in which the hand is grasped.

Never before did I see such unmistakable evidence of sympathy and friendship, as gushed from those rustic faces. Had they been as mute as the trees around, we would willingly have placed our case in their hands.

"You say you are very hungry," added Juan, with a significant look at Florence, who sprang away like an arrow down the mountain, over rocks and logs, through brush and bushes she bounded like a stricken doe, and was in a few moments lost to sight.

While Florence was gone Juan, who principally did the talking, proceeded to tell us, first, how we were beset with dangers, and how she thought she could extricate us. If we would entirely submit our case into her hands, do just as she directed, in all things, she would undertake to lead us from the mountain and conceal us until she could find a guide to go with us to Knoxville: that she had had much experience in hiding her brother and other friends, and knew no doubt, much more about what was necessary, and where to put us, than we; and that she could not undertake it if there was to be any conflict of authority; that she would imperil their safety by taking ours in charge; that they were surrounded by rebels, and already suspicioned of being decidedly in sympathy with the Federal Government, and watched by every rebel in the neighborhood.

We did not hesitate to answer them that we placed the entire matter in their charge, and that we would not exercise any will of our own, without their direction or approval.

Florence in the meantime, had returned to us with a basket of provisions, which, though homely, I remember as being the most delicious food that was ever my fortune to eat, especially the corn cakes, in a triangular shape, about two inches thick, and yet a little warm from dinner, when laid open and liberally spread with butter and molasses, were good enough even for Cleopatra. And the large red apples, large as a tin cup, that Florence passed us, in her apron, were of such a quality that none but starving men can fully appreciate.

After a stay of nearly an hour, the girls left us, with the understanding that they were to return again at dark and take us from that mountain, to some better and more comfortable place of concealment.

CHAPTER VI.

THE WOMEN OF NORTH CAROLINA—WAITING FOR GUIDES—THE CANDY PULLING—THE OLD GOSSIPS—MORE FEMALE STRATEGY — ADIEUS — AMONG THE ROBBERS—THEIR MURDERS—THEIR CAVE—THEIR ENGAGEMENT WITH US—WHY THEY HAD TO TARRY—THE EXPEDITION TO DR. —— —THE CAPTURE OF ONE OF THE VANCES—OUR HURRIED DEPARTURE—CROSSING THE FRENCH BROAD RIVER—GOOD AND HIS PONE—BANKS BURTON'S—HIS NEIGHBORS AND FAMILY—AMONG THE MOUNTAINS—THE OBSTINACY OF OUR GUIDES—THE MAJESTY OF MOUNT PISGAH—ABANDONED BY OUR GUIDES IN THE WILD MOUNTAINS.

We were much relieved by this accidental meeting. No one of our party was unkind enough to entertain even a thought of infidelity in the girls. Their manner of expression and action, though not half so emphatic and full of show as better educated folks, yet they had in them such simplicity, such naturalness, such freedom from deceit, that every word they uttered was believed.

So, we had really found the "good Union people" of North Carolina, to whom we had looked with so much hope. The clouds of difficulty that had gathered about us that day, so thick and dreadful, were but the darkness preceeding the light of the morning. We considered no probabilities, felt no scruples, but awaited as confidently the return of our benefactress, as the child would wait for its mother.

A little after dark, two of the girls came slipping noiselessly up the mountain. They had arranged to take us to the garret of their dwelling, and told us this kind of a story about their old father: Said he was an old man, and loved the Union, but they lived in a rebel neighborhood and were tenants to a rebel landlord; that he had been two or three times arrested upon suspicion of harboring rebel deserters and refugees, and if anything should come of our concealment in their house, they much desired that their father be able to swear that he knew nothing at all about it, and in view of these facts they would enjoin upon us the most perfect quiet when he was about the house.

A reasonable story; and we believed it at the time, but it afterwards came to our knowledge, by third parties, that their father was a bitter rebel.

Juan instructed us that we should follow thirty paces behind her and her sister, and if we heard a certain signal from her, as, "*Who are you?*" all must quickly hide.

Down the mountain we crept, shivering and shaking with the cold. Over the fence into the field, stooping forward, by the direction of Juan, so that the fence would cover us, we thus hurried across, to an old stable filled with fodder, and perhaps a hundred yards from the house. In the corner of this stable we crouched, and the girls, calling up Tige, their fierce dog, hastened into the house with him.

Another moment and fleet-footed Florence came tripping to us with the unwelcome intelligence, that a company of neighbors, all rebels, were in the house, and that we would have to remain yet a little longer in the fodder.

Another few minutes and Florence came gliding in again, like a spirit, with a pot of rye coffee she had managed to make. After having drank the hot coffee, we really seemed colder than before. We were so exceeding chilled that our teeth pounded each other till our very jaws ached. Chisman afterwards affirmed to the girls that he had to stick his head in a crack of the stable to keep his jaws from shaking out his teeth.

Soon after Florence went back, the old dog got out of the house and set up a fearful barking and snuffing of the air, in the direction of our retreat. Their father and Juan came rushing out of the house at the same time, the father remarking:

"Juan, what in the world can this dog be barking at so?"

"Oh," said she, "I guess he's only mad because somebody has turned him out into the cold—it's too bad for the old fellow to have to stay out all this cold night—so, Tige, come back into the house—poor fellow," and they all walked in together.

The girls seemed much more exercised for our comfort than we were ourselves. In fact our prospects had been so improved under the new dispensation, that we came near forgetting that we were cold.

About ten o'clock Caroline came to us and said they had arranged to take us into the house at once, as their visitors would probably stay till midnight; that when we heard them commence singing at the house, we must pull off our boots and slip, one at a time, to the house, and up stairs and into the left hand room as quietly as possible, and should they suddenly hush singing, if any one was coming he must retreat again to the stable. We pulled off our boots and made ourselves ready for the signal.

Soon there broke from the house such a strain of melodies as is never heard away from the mountains, loud, clear and vigorous, ringing and swelling out upon the air like the chiming of bells in a steeple, the words chosen being Mr. Hart's old familiar hymn, "Come, you sinners, poor and needy." One by one we shot up to the house, and as I bounded along, I could but smile to hear the words of the old song, never before appreciated, and which seemed fully as appropriate to the occasion as true. Up the stairs we went, and into the room as directed, and there, "God bless the women, every one," in the absence of a stove, sat a big iron kettle full of hot coals. As soon as we were housed above, one of the girls sang out, in the hall below:

"Oh, let's quit this; it's so cold it don't pay, unless the folks would give more attention to us;" and into the room they broke, complaining and scolding their visitors for their indifference to a nice serenade.

Our room was small and close, and the kettle of coals soon made it comfortable. Down upon the floor we sat, around the kettle, as noiseless as could be desired.

So far so good, and our sad condition a few hours before was past ameliorating, though it was hard for us to appreciate that we were still among our enemies and yet among our friends; that many of the hearts of that Sunday night party, making merry below, would be appalled if they knew that four Yankees rested above them in the same house; and yet four of them, ostensibly the merriest of all, were in painful suspense for the rest to go home, that they might resume their ministrations of mercy.

Fun went on down stairs till after eleven o'clock before the neighbors took their leave. Then in a few minutes the girls came tearing up stairs as if to bed, blustered around awhile in their own chamber, then came tip-toe-ing it in their stocking feet into ours. Also in their old mother's heart the germ of loyalty was still quick and green, and when she saw their father in bed she too slipped up stairs, squeezed our hands, bade us welcome to her house, and went down to bed.

The four girls sat up with us an hour later, and you timid Indiana girls will not believe me, perhaps, when I say that after midnight two of them walked alone, three miles and back, through the wild woods, in quest of the guides they had promised us.

This is one of many examples we saw there of what woman can perform when she has a mind to do and a heart to brave. Think of it, philanthropic ladies of Indiana! How many of you so loved the late soldiers that you would dare the midnight ghosts and freezing elements for two hours, as these two did, in a country beset with robbers and rebels, for the mere accommodation of four strange, unseemly men, and that, too, without a request? How many of you would assume the danger of being locked up in jail, or banished from your homes in order to protect and conceal four men, bound to you with no stronger ties than the common relation we all bear to our Creator? How many of you would be willing to lay aside your flowers or your embroidery to go into the woods to cut and haul wood, or to make rails to fence a field the enemy had laid waste, or to plow or to sow wheat, or to harvest, or to carry a half bushel of corn or wheat on your shoulder five miles to mill, and then having baked it into bread, carry it the same distance after dark to your father, husband, or brother, who was hiding out in the mountains, living in caves to keep out of the rebel army, and from fighting against a government he loved? Yet the loyal North Carolina women, created in the same likeness and strength, during the war did all these things, and more, without a murmur.

Juan said of the guides they expected to find us:

"Gentlemen, they are bad men, at least they are so regarded by both rebels and Unionists; they have the reputation of killing many people and robbing many more; they have been declared outlaws by the proper authorities, and one thousand dollars reward offered for their arrest. They have been several times through the mountains to Knoxville, and are well acquainted with the way, besides they will be as cautious, on account of their own safety, as anybody in whose care you can be placed. But you should never be captured with them; their lives are forfeited, and it would not be wise for you to consider your lives worth anything if found in the company of Jack and Jerry Vance."

As soon as the girls came into our room, they blinded the single window with a heavy quilt and lighted a candle. I at once looked pryingly around for a way to the garret or closet, and seeing none, I turned and whispered to Juan:

"Why, certainly, this cannot be that fine place to hide you spoke about?"

"Now, sir," she replied, a little jocosely, "ask no more questions about that, if you please; we understand that you have submitted that matter altogether to us."

Feeling a little rebuked, I said no more upon that subject.

There was a bed in this room, the stead being very plain, with a staff set in the top of each post, extending up near the ceiling, and over the top of which staffs was stretched a sheet of white muslin, so near the color and lying so near the plastering, that it required a close look to discover it. I, however, noticed it, and fostered a lurking suspicion that that sheet had something to do in our concealment. Time wore on in general conversation till Juan spoke:

"Mary, come here," and they took hold of the ends of the bed and slid it along the floor, and which carried the sheet along and uncovered a snug little scuttle hole leading to the garret. They then explained the arrangement. It had been prepared entirely by their own hands to conceal their brother from the rebel conscripting officers, and in which they succeeded for nine weeks, when the confinement became so unbearable that he came out of his own accord, and gave himself up and went to the army, preferring it to garret life or roaming in the mountains.

Mary, springing upon the bed, reached into the garret and drew therefrom a light ladder, and made it ready for our ascent. Then said she, "If you will go up that ladder you will find a bed made down for you, with, perhaps, plenty of cover." We went up, drew the ladder after us and back went the sheet again over the hole. Above we found a comfortable bed, made for the occasion, and slept soundly the balance of the night.

The next morning, when their father had gone to his work, the girls came again up stairs, and after a little preparation below, again removed the sheet and invited us out of the garret. When we went down we found a kettle of fresh coals, some water and towels, and a good breakfast smoking upon the table.

It was now that we learned that the two girls who had been in search of our guides had failed to find them, but had learned that they were at the time out of the county, and would not return for three or four days, and may be a week. Their friends, however, had sent us assurance that the boys would undertake to guide us to Knoxville, if we would wait till they came back. So stay right there we must was the order, and we rather liked the plan since we had to be delayed.

For four days and nights we remained in that house,

staying the most of the time by day in the room we first entered, unless their father or some rebel visitor was about the house; then we were sent to the garret.

The girls, like most of their gender, could not keep their secret. Every Union girl for miles around, and there were a good many, had intelligence of us in twenty-four hours, and they were curious there as here. A new one was coming in almost every hour to see that wonderful creature, a live Yankee. And one man, who had for many years been a cripple, and whose heart had remained right, was also brought in to have a "little talk." This gentleman, as well to show his hospitality as to sharpen up our wits and loosen up our tongues, carried in with him a bottle of North Carolina Tonic, which, in justice to the occasion, I must say went not away dishonored. It was this man who first leaked out the secret that the father of the girls was a rebel in principle, and a bitter one at that.

Unfortunately for the family they had had no advantages in education, and no one of them could read or write. They had a good many absent friends, and among them an only brother and two brothers-in-law in the rebel army. They required of us to write for them a letter to every one, and read one they had had from their brother nearly two weeks.

Out of this letter writing liked to have come trouble, but only came another example of their ready sagacity and invention. One morning after their father had gone, as we all thought, to haul wood for an ex-Confederate cabinet officer, I had occasion to go down stairs after a bottle of ink that I knew to be there; and while returning, and about half way up the stairs, some one opened the door behind me, and supposing it one of the girls I stopped and looked round, and, to my great surprise, saw their father face to face. One more bound and I was at the top of the stairs, and into the room, full of perplexity.

The old man, going into the room below, asked, "Juan, what man was that I saw going up stairs?"

Juan broke out into a violent laugh, in which her mother and sister joined, and replied, "Why that was nobody but Florence; she put on a suit of Dave's clothes to haul wood in, and ran up stairs when she saw you coming."

They effectually laughed the old man into the belief that it was Florence, and soon he went off, giving himself no further trouble about it.

On the fourth day of our stay with these good people, the sister of our expected guides came over and told us that her brothers had returned, and that they would see us that night in the mountains, and that she and her lady friend had come to lead us to them. A very foolish notion took possession of our girls and these two, for they held that we should not leave their house without some kind of social frolic, and they had decided on a candy pulling. We did not like the idea, but raised no serious objection.

Accordingly when night came they built up two big fires below, one in each room, put on a gallon of sorghum, and thus began the preliminaries.

About this time there appeared at the gate an old woman, a perfect old gossip, who, from reputation, was never happy only when talking of the adversity of some of her neighbors. A regular run-about-everywhere-and-tattle; and she was a rebel, too. The old woman walked into the house and very sedately began to inquire about the health of a little grandchild in the family.

"Sick!"

"Yes; aint Jakey sick?"

Its mother, suspecting somebody had been lying to the

old woman, to settle her curiosity, began: "Well, I do declare, grandmother, there is something remarkable about Jakey; this afternoon about four o'clock he got right up out of the cradle, and has been running around ever since, as if nothing had ever been the matter with him. Did you ever hear tell of the like, grandmother? I am really scared about him."

The old woman examined the child's pulse, pronounced it very unnatural, said he had some fever, and looked so bad; while in truth the child had not been sick a moment in a month. It was all explained when Elizabeth Vance told how the old woman had asked her and Matilda Pewitt what they were running over to —— so much for, and that she had told her that little Jakey was very sick.

She had come to stay all night with the sick, and much trouble she gave to the girls in their candy pulling. She insisted on staying in the room with them, rather than go into the other room where the old folks were. She wanted to see if they pulled candy now, like they did when she was a girl. She hadn't seen the like for so long. But the girls, getting a little vexed at her perverseness, plainly asked her to go into the other house, as they wished to have a little private fun of their own.

This was a triumph, and they soon had us below, the door locked, the window blinded, one of the girls on picket outside, and the wax sticking to every finger in the room. We pulled so much Sorghum wax at Columbia, that we were adepts in the business. The science with which we jerked it was astonishing to the girls; but when Chisman, in showing them a touch of a Columbia professionalist, got a half pound of soft wax in his hair, I thought Florence would go into spasms.

It was the desire to keep our fun quiet, but sufficient noise reached the ears of the unwelcome visitor in the other room to arouse her suspicion, and she inquired if she did not hear men's voices somewhere. Our good mother assured her that she heard nothing but the girls, and then stepped out into the yard to tell the picket to caution us to be stiller. The caution was communicated, but we soon forgot it, and made perhaps more noise than before. Again we were heard by the old gossip, and again she declared that she heard men's voices, and that she was going in the other room to see if there were not some at the candy party. The mother begged her not to do it, that it would make the girls mad, she knew, if she disturbed them in their fun. Again the sentinel was visited, and instructed to advise us to depart, for the old woman would surely find us out soon if that noise prevailed.

Immediately, upon this intelligence, we dropped our candy and began preparations to leave our benefactresses.

I shall never forget that parting. It was not in tears, nor in multitudinous acknowledgments, but there was a gratitude felt and a sympathy reciprocated that marks but few occasions. They had found us in the last moments of expiring hope. They had attended us for four days with more than sisterly care, and had rebuilt us with a new life and a new hope. All that we left in return, or could leave, was a written certificate of their treatment, signed with our names in full, and rank, to show our soldiers, if they ever came among them, that they were friendly to our cause even when the rebels were in power.

Elizabeth Vance and her cousin, who had come to conduct us to the guides, led off toward the Blue Ridge. The excitement created by our debut at Flat Rock having now subsided, it was not thought necessary by our guides to observe special caution, as our way lay over an unfrequented trail through the woods. In fact we had no time to look or listen if we kept up with the girls, for they hurried along with a speed I never could understand. They could jump a bigger branch and walk a smaller log than any of us; could get up a clift or over a fence while we would be studying how.

It took us but a few minutes to get over the three miles that brought us to the foot of the Blue Ridge, and to the place where we expected to find Jack and Jerry Vance. It was in the angle of intersecting roads, fast asleep upon their guns, under an oak tree, that we found them. As we approached near, rustling the leaves a little, they both instantly sprang to their feet, with their guns in their hands, and in a coarse voice commanded: "Halt! Who comes there?"

Their sister's voice was satisfactory.

If any reader should be curious to know the general appearance of these men, I would say, first fix in your mind an untutored man, thirty-five years old, standing six feet high, in a suit of coarse home-made jeans; his skin dark, but not as dark as his long hair that grew down almost to his eyes, nor as dark as his beard that covered most of his face; his black eyes set deep in his head, under a pair of heavy, closely knitted brows, and though seldom fixed directly at you, his glare when it did come was withering. Now fix his wool hat all full of holes, and his Springfield rifle bright as steel can be laying across his left arm with his right hand hold of the hammer and trigger, and it will do for the form of Jerry Vance.

Then a younger man, but twenty-one years old with shorter hair, beardless, and in most ways a more honest looking man than his brother; more stoutly built though not so tall, a milder eye, a more intelligent look, and but for his talk you would fail to take him for as bad a man as he is; and this will be enough to say to gather the outlines of Jack Vance.

When we went up they spoke not a word to us, but sharply said:

"Liz., who are these men you bring here?"

"Why, Jerry, these are the Yankees who have been over at —— these four days."

"How in the —— do you know they are Yankees?"

"Say," turning to us now, "we want to know just who you are, and how you came in this country?"

We, a little agitated, proceeded to give him the facts. "Were you ever in the rebel service?"

"No."

"Where do you live?" and so on through a most rigid examination, then extending his gun he added: "Lay your hands upon this gun and swear that you have told me the truth in every syllable, or we'll shoot you upon the spot."—Clap went four hands down upon the cold steel.—"You swear that you have told us the truth in all things, and this you do on the penalty of being shot the moment we find out to the contrary?"

"Girls, go home—meet us at the Devil's Boot at sun up in the morning with breakfast for six. Jack, give these men a drink from the canteen. Strangers, sit down by this tree and tell us what you want."

Having received such uniform kind words and kind treatment from our female friends, this unexpected severity made us all devoutly wish that we had never seen the Vances, and we came near being unkind enough to blame those who had placed us in their hands. They looked so much like rebel soldiers with their guns in their hands, and they talked so much like our first captors, and then it was painfully evident that they were not much interested in our behalf.

Negotiations began at once, which in an hour resulted in a contract that they should guide us to Knoxville, nearly two hundred miles by the mountains, for four hundred dollars, payable in gold and silver. We acquiesced in the price much sooner than in the delay of a week, which they thought probably necessary for them to make ready for the expedition. We could imagine but little cause of delay in men of their reputed occupation—hiding from the rebels—and the uncertainty they expressed as to the time they would be able to start was altogether unsatisfactory, but as there seemed no alternative we agreed to wait.

When a full understanding was reached it was one o'clock in the morning, and it being cold and frosty we yet walked two miles to somebody's stable loft where we all slept till the chickens began crowing for day, then we crawled out, having first turned the hay over to leave no sign, and wended our way two and a half miles up into the mountain to the Devil's Boot, where we were to have our breakfasts.

About the appointed hour, Elizabeth, with two or three neighbor girls, came to us in accordance with orders, with a bountiful supply of provision. Their mother came to us about noon, and she was our frequent visitor during the three days that we staid in the neighborhood. She was much pleased in the arrangement we had made with her boys, for she had long been urging them to go to Knoxville to spend the winter; said she saw no chance for them to stay at home and escape capture on account of the snow. It was from her that we learned more about her boys than from any body else. Their life at the time was something of this nature: They both had deserted places in the rebel army, and it one day leaked out accidentally that Jack had also but recently deserted the Union army, the Second North Carolina, recruited at Knoxville. They had now resolved to turn the war to their advantage, to use their own words, since they were driven from their domestic pursuits by rebels they would make rebels pay their wages. Six others, similarly circumstanced, were acting with them in their work and defense. They expressed the most inveterate hate for rebels, and whether true or false, scrupulously regarded every man a rebel who had valuables. They now lived on spoils, or rather hoped to live on them, for it was the business of the gang to roam the country over for many miles, sacking every "fine house," and it was on an expedition of this sort that they were absent when we first met the girls in the mountain. Something to eat was the least consideration, as they only occasionally took a ham or some luxuries. Money was their principal object, but they never left behind jewelry and silver ware—of the latter they had accumulated an abundance, from teaspoons to milk pitchers, the value of which I can give no estimate, but they always spoke of it as a life-time competency when they should find a market. They had a cave in the mountains, where they staid in bad weather, and where they stored their plunder; and to look around the dingy walls of that damp den, and see here and there suspended on a stick in a crevice, collections of costly service, all cankered and black, you could hardly believe that they were but a short time ago the dazzling splendor of hospitable boards. But the strangest thing was the life-size oil painting of Washington that stood in one end, which was really worth a hundred dollars, but which could have been bought from the present owners for fifty cents. When asked what they wanted with such property as that, they answered:

"We found the old gentlemen in the society of rebels, and we thought he would be happier in the cave of a Union man than in the parlor of a rebel."

They had lived in the mountains for two years, excepting the three months that Jack had spent in the Union army at Knoxville, and they had not slept in a house or eaten from a table in the time—regular wild men—making their shoes in the mountains for themselves and friends out of leather they had stolen from the tanner.

There were many such gangs as this in the mountain districts of the South during the war; or, not exactly *such* gangs, but men who banded together and lived in the mountains to keep out of the rebel army. Generally these gangs were composed of as loyal, generous-hearted, honest men as the country has in it—men with a common cause and a common aim, never in feuds nor crimes, but homogeneous and harmonious as a brigade, collecting together occasionally for a more powerful defense.

But this was not the case with the Vance gang. They were at war with all the rest. Their depredations were so notorious that the rebel authorities had published a solemn proclamation of out-lawry against them, as well as increase their force and diligence against all other men who were lying out in the mountains.

Thus, by the outrages of this gang, the good men who were dodging from the army, out of loyal and patriotic motives, were much more harrassed than they would have been, and a united effort in the neighboring gangs to restrain them in their lawlessness, had resulted in a brisk skirmish, but a few weeks before we saw them, in which one of the gang had been badly wounded.

Like us, the mother of Jerry and Jack, could not understand what business they had that need delay them a week. She knew of no business they had but to eat, sleep and hide. But the boys insisted that they had something to arrange. So anxious were we to be off, and so much concerned was their mother about their safety, that we jointly besieged them, night and day, to go or tell the cause of delay.

Jerry, the second day, a little bit fretted, said, "Well, if you must know the reason, it is this: Dr. —— has got one hundred and two dollars in silver, and I'll be —— if I leave this part of the country till we get it. The Dr. is not home now, and will probably not be back for a week."

This explanation was not satisfactory to us. We held a little conference aside and decided to put an end to the delay by increasing their compensation one hundred and two dollars. It took us but a moment to decide upon this; and if the sum had been a thousand dollars, it would have been as readily pledged. Time had no measure of value with us then; the pressure of circumstance was so great that every penny we could command, or could hope to command upon our arrival at Knoxville, would have been pledged, no doubt, for a single twenty-four hours.

But our spirits fell again, when Jerry rejected our proposition, saying that they had their minds made up about the silver, and would not change them, and when we grew perhaps a little importune in the matter, the same man very ungenerously replied, "if you men can't wait till we get ready to go, I advise you to put on at once without us." Only that there was no alternative, we consented to wait. Yes, wait, and to appear a little more patient in it, too, for we could see clearly through their careless and crusty answers, that they were not the least enthusiastic in their engagement with us, and our fears were, that if they had but little discouragement, they would abandon it. So, after this interview, we at once became complaisant—yes, radically so—never disputed with them any more, and actually studied their pleasure with care, as much to keep them in the notion of Knoxville, as to keep their good will. And this latter was by no means undesirable, for, notwithstanding their extreme abuse of rebels, we were just about as afraid of them as we were of the rebel soldiers.

Matters went on tediously enough till the third day, about noon, when the news reached us, through Elizabeth, that the subject of our delay had returned home. Consequently Jerry sent Jack to the top of a mountain to fire two shots, one from a musket and one from a rifle, which was the signal for the assembling of the gang at the cave.

The first one to report, about the middle of the afternoon, was Sam Johnson, a man of thirty, wearing a cap made by himself from a red fox skin, with the full tail hanging down behind. Soon afterwards came Dick Duncan and Tim Tansell. I pitied bright-eyed, innocent-looking young Duncan, who evidently belonged to better society, and to a more honest business, but I never had a doubt that coarse, orangoutang-looking Tim Tansell was not in his natural element. If stealing is innate in anybody, there could have been nothing abnormal about this man's tendencies, for no one with honest instincts could put on such a hideous costume as he had the courage to wear. On his head he wore a striped turban, rolled up all round, and a half dozen long, black chicken feathers set in the top. His coat, or jacket, was made out of the skin of a bear dressed with the hair on, and so arranged that the fore legs formed the sleeves and the paws the cuffs, hanging down over the hands, showing the claws of the veritable animal. Around the irregular collar, and gathered into a great bow-knot in front, was bound the unseemly spotted skin of a rattlesnake.

Mike Hedge and Jim Beck sat down with us about five o'clock, but it was sun down before Gus Ives got in. They all carried their guns and some articles of dress that would change their general appearance.

The object of the summons was soon explained to be Dr. ——'s $102 of silver, and met with the hearty concurrence of every one present.

But there was one thing we did not all agree to, and that was the request they made of us four, to take guns and go with them. Against this we protested most earnestly. We had in us no spirit for pillage. We felt no desire for the romance of robbing, and, probably, murdering; and our zeal in begging was all the more animated when they brought out four rusty guns and said we had to go. Young Duncan was enlisted in our behalf, and urged upon his companions the injustice and impropriety of making us go against our will; said we could very truly have no interest in the matter—that we could not wish to punish and rob a man that had done us no harm; that there were plenty of them for the work, and it was unnecessary as it was unjust to impose upon us the hazard of the outlaw's penalty by engaging in that expedition. His timely intercessions succeeded in having us excused from going, but did not protect us from a most intolerant abusing, and unwarranted insinuations that we were rebel spies. One man was detailed to stay with us, and at dark the other seven men, blacked and muffled, were on their way to Dr. ——'s.

The result of the expedition we have only from them, as gathered from a random conversation among themselves next morning These are about the facts, as we understood them. When they reached the house of the Dr., he and his family were still sitting around the fire, unsuspectingly enough. The ruffians marched up near the window and, without the least notice, fired a full volley directly into the family circle; then charged into the house with empty guns. Fortunately no one was hit, and more fortunately still, the Doctor had escaped by running out the back way into the woods. Upon entering, they found none but the wife and three daughters, in mortal terror, and answering that the old gentleman was not about the house, they proceeded to ransack it from cellar to garret. Under the beds, up stairs, they found three negro men concealed, as much frightened as the ladies. Satisfied that the doctor was not about the house, they then took their rope which they had for the purpose, and tied it around the wife's neck and threatened to hang her if some of them did not tell where the hundred and two dollars in silver was. In this they failed, but only abandoned their inhuman treatment after one or two of the girls had fainted with fright.

Having failed to get the money, they were determined they would not fail in their barbarous fun, so they brought in the three negro men, whom they had taken from under the bed, in the sitting room, in the presence of the ladies, and made one pat and the other two dance for their amusement. As cruel as was the treatment, it was hard to prevent a smile to hear those wild men talk about how they made those negroes dance for their lives. They made them dance with all their energies, for a straight hour, without one moment's cessation, and when from exhaustion they would moderate their activity a little, the heartless bystanders would bring down their guns and command them to "go into it, or we'll shoot you in a minute." Thus they kept him at it, till they both sunk to the floor. Tired of this, they plundered the bureau and cupboard and retired.

Early next morning Dr. ——, hied off to Hendersonville and told the story of his outrage to the commander of a regiment of militia stationed there, whereupon the entire regiment was transported in wagons, in great haste, to our community to hunt out the offenders. The first we knew of this movement was about eleven o'clock in the morning. At this time we were impatiently lounging on the side of the mountain, near the cave, waiting for a decision from our guides, now that they had failed in their attempt to get the silver, when we saw the mother coming running towards the cave without bonnet and with disheveled hair, crying and calling Jerry. The militia had made a *coup de main* into that vicinity and had really captured their brother, living four miles off, and had tied him, hands and feet, and thrown him into a wagon like a hog, to be hauled to execution at Hendersonville.

The event was probably a lucky one for us, for it frightened the boys, and from the outcries of the mother, they consented to start at once for Knoxville, or as soon as they could possibly get provisions enough for the trip, which would require ten days. The mother gave directions to be ready to start at three o'clock in the evening, and to go at once two miles further into the mountains to a certain "cove," and that she would get the help of her neighbors and meet us in the cove at the appointed time, with all the provisions that we required.

After making some hasty dispositions about the cave, and hiding their favorite guns in a hollow tree to keep the rust from ruining them, each buckled two revolvers around his waist and set out with us.

It was hard to tell now who of us was the most anxious for three o'clock and the meat and bread. Every few minutes one of them would go to the mountain summit to look and listen. Soon after three o'clock the mother was with us again more frightened and distressed than before, for in the meantime the militia had searched the house and stable; and had taken every mouthful of meat and nearly all the bread she had prepared. What corn bread two of the neighbors had furnished and a little dried beef was all she brought, and among the rest was one corn pone which contained exactly a peck of meal, that Jane Howard had borrowed and baked for the occasion.

Soon after four o'clock of that afternoon we turned our backs to that people with few regrets. Though the women had been uniformly kind to us, yet there prevailed among them such a spirit of ruffianism, and such uncivilized manners, that our stay among them was everything but agreeable.

Again under way for home, and this time behind two experienced guides, our hopes of success grew lively, too lively for the pleasure of our guides, for we would crowd upon their heels and get sent back every few minutes with some terrible oath. At dark we went down off the mountains and took the road, to enable us to make seventeen miles that night to a brother-in-law's of Jerry, where we expected to complete our supply of provisions.

Nine miles ahead was the French Broad, and in crossing the river we anticipated some trouble. Our only hope was in finding one of two canoes, reported to be hidden along its banks. The river at this point was deep and rough which made it very dangerous to swim, or to attempt to cross on a poorly constructed raft. Up and down the banks of the noisy stream we wandered for half an hour, hunting for the canoes without success, and our guides decided that before we would risk a swim or a temporary raft that we would go four miles up the river and cross on an old bridge there. When we reached the place we found nothing of a bridge but two rows of piles stretching across the river, with 18 inch sleepers lying on the tops of each row. The rest of the bridge, years before had been swept away by high waters, and there had been no steps taken to rebuild it. To cross over these sleepers seemed practicable, so down on our hands and knees we got and crawled upon them. Though a little nervous all the while, we got along admirably till within thirty or forty feet of the opposite shore when, behold, to our great discomfiture some ruthless hand had rolled a sleeper from each row into the river. This was too bad, within thirty or forty feet of the other side and yet too far to get over. For several minutes we sat in a quandary not knowing whether to retrace or sit there wishing. In the meantime we discovered that the sleeper which had been rolled off above still lay beneath against the piles with one end on some driftwood on the shore. Baker who happened to be in front, and there was no changing about on that narrow log, concluded that he would swing under and slide down the pile to the water and examine the feasibility of getting over on the floating log. Under he swings, down the pile he glides, plants his foot cautiously on the log, into the water it goes, Baker sticking bravely to it until he is buoyed, then he lets go the pile, makes one step forward and another and another, and by the time he reaches the next pile he is raised almost entirely out of the water and walks triumphantly to the other side. Now that Baker was over, all must be, and as he had crossed on the floating log all could cross, so at it we went in turns. All were soon on the other side but the Irishman, he was not so successful. I have neglected to mention that he was the custodian of the peck pone of bread and that was all the provisions he carried, and that was more than his share even then, but because he was tough and willing we were disposed to place the honorable duty upon him. He carried his charge in a haversack prepared by the donor of the bread, and which in strength and capacity was equal to the burden.

Good was behind and when the rest of us all got to the other side, there he sat on top holding tenaciously to the sleeper, and the big pone holding to him, insisting that it was no use trying for he knew that he could not cross on that tottering log. Generally he was the bravest of the party, but some how or other he had an aversion for water that was marked the whole trip. We promised to help him with a pole, still he could not be persuaded, and becoming a little vexed we threatened to stone him off the sleeper if he did not try, for we could not be delayed there all night by his cowardice. He would much rather have charged a battery than attempted that crossing, but when we alluded to his cowardice he was decided upon drowning or reaching the bank. Quick as a sailor could have done it, he was under the sleeper clinging like a flying-squirrel with his short legs and arms to the pile, down he slips a little piece and, Holy St. Patrick! there lay the monstrous pone still on top, and the string of his haversack fast on a splinter. He asserted that he would strip it off his houlder and let it go—we declared we would drown him if he did. He was in great distress but concealed it like a stoic. Again he pulls himself up the pile an inch at a time till he reaches the sleeper; now he holds on with his legs and one hand and employs the other in assisting down the pone. Cautiously he proceeds, but in an unguarded moment the unrighteous pone comes tumbling off and jerks the unhappy boy down the pile into the water to his neck. If we had not felt concerned about his life sure enough now we would have been unable to render any assistance for laughter, but as it was Chisman ran out on the floating log with a long pole and soon had our unfortunate comrade wringing his clothes on the bank, and another item to laugh about at our leisure.

We had yet eight miles to go to reach the brother-inaws', and as it was our desire to make that distance before daylight we tarried no longer than was necessary to wring our clothes and pour the water out of our boots. Our guides being fresh and skilled in night walking moved along briskly, and continued through the entire eight miles without stopping a moment to rest.

"The honest watch dog" bayed at us at Banks Burton's before the chickens called out the morning. The family were all asleep, but through Jerry we soon got a welcome admission into the house. Chisman did honest Mr. Burton the honor to ask if the promise to Abraham had been repeated to him, that if he would depart into a strange land he should become the father of a great nation. And truly the facts seemed to warrant such an inquiry. The cabin of but one room, the fruitful home of the latter days patriarch, we found sitting down between two mountains in the midst of a farm of just seven acres, boasting the very "magnicentfi distance" of six mountain miles to the nearest neighbors. Upon entering the house it had more the appearance of an infantry hospital than anything else. There were two beds on steads, "and pallets to the right of us, pallets to the left of us, pallets all around," with children in regular ratio from one to twenty-one resting upon them. It was with difficulty that we crowded our way through and arranged ourselves on an old bench before the fireplace, occupying nearly all one end of the house. If it was only the hospitable nature of our host that prompted him to such an exertion for our comfort and pleasure, we have few such in Indiana. Having first built us a good fire, he then went to the bed on steads and turning out three large girls, insisted that we four strangers occupy the same for sleep the balance of the morning. This we did not wish to do. Men of our habits, with wet and dirty clothes would vastly prefer sleeping on the floor before the fire, and we told the old gentleman so, but the more we would excuse ourselves the more he would insist that he had plenty of girls that could wash easier than we could lay on puncheons.

Next morning the family were up early, big and little, crowding and whispering that four Yankees were " asleep in that bed." "Does they look like pap?" said one little urchin to his mother.

"Do Yankees kill little boys?" concerned another young hopeful, and a fourth wanted to know, " will they kill Abraham Lambe ?" a rebel he knew of.

It will be remembered it was the arrangement to increase our supply of provisions at this place fully one-half, and strange to say, we found this enormous family without a mouthful of meat or an ounce of breadstuff in the house, and they talked of the circumstance as nothing uncommon. The nearest mill was twelve miles, and the nearest neighbor six, but soon after sun-up two boys got in with a half bushel of borrowed meal. In the meantime our two guides and the host had gone to the mountain ranges for meat, and soon after the boys returned. They came down the mountain, dragging after them two considerable hogs they had killed. These hogs they dressed like beeves at the foot of the mountain, and carried the meat to the house on poles.

At eight o'clock breakfast was in process of preparation; at nine it was ready and we called to eat. The breakfast consisted only of coffee made from parched meal, corn bread and fresh pork. If I have to tell it all, too, I will have to say that their entire table service consisted of six plates, including two tin pans, three knives, two forks, and one large, antediluvian dish. Not one single cup or saucer made its appearance, but gourds answered in their stead. This seemed like true poverty indeed, yet we heard less complaint about hard times than by many well to do families in this State of plenty and influence,—yes, saw more generous hospitality, a greater willingness to divide a scanty subsistence with a needy fellow creature, than we could hope to find in a majority of families around us in Indiana. For, notwithstanding Mr. Burton's poverty, notwithwithstanding his humble walk in life and modest pretensions, there was in his heart that spirit of brotherly love and godly charity, that should entitle him to a higher social standard in the estimation of a Christian people, than the thousands of sordid rich who hoard up for decay, and turn the needy away empty. It is among such untutored poor that we find truly the normal condition of man, and it is from such that we can best learn the strange but unequivocal fact, that education, refinement and wealth, with their attendant blessings, have withal a tendency to alienate the heart from its natural and christian duties. Riches and rebellion, poverty and loyalty, were correlative terms in the South during the war.

This family prepared us a large quantity of meat and what bread they could spare, and had us ready to resume our journey by eleven o'clock. But for some reason our guides were disposed to be tardy, and it was late in the afternoon before we left Mr. Burton's. Then when we did leave it was in a slow and careless manner, resting every half mile longer than it took us to walk that distance; but what troubled us most were the frequent private interviews and whisperings of our guides. Matters went on till night in a very unsatisfactory manner, the time being spent without a half dozen words being interchanged between us and those upon whom we so much depended. Next morning it was long after sun-up before we got started. Jack now feigned sickness, and Jerry continued to talk discouragingly of the prospects; he had heard of so many perishing in the snow; our way lay over the roughest of the range one hundred and eighty miles, and the clouds betokened snow already; we had not half enough food for the trip, etc., etc.

All day long very much disheartened we trudged along, up and down, up and down, the mountain peaks and succeeded just before the sun set in reaching the summit of Mount Pisgah, reputed among the natives of Western North Carolina as being the second highest mountain in all the Appalachian range, and from whose summit the eye can see into five States, namely, North Carolina, South Carolina, Georgia, Tennessee and Virginia. From this mountain, directly in our course, apparently within a mile and a half, but which in reality was seven miles away, we saw a number of mysterious fires. The guides became more uneasy than ever at the appearance of these fires. They withdrew and consulted twenty minutes; then climbed a tree and averred that they could see men moving about the fires seven miles off, and that they knew no other route than over that particular mountain. They also pathetically spoke of the outlaw's penalty, and the terrible result if they were to be captured, and were of the opinion that no rational man would try to pass that mountain with the indications of danger that they could so clearly see; and further, as for them they would, from no inducements, attempt it now, but if we would return home with them and stay through the winter, the next spring they would be sure to take us through for half the compensation. No anticipated danger could dissuade us from our purpose of going ahead, for dangers were all around us, behind us and on all sides, apparently equal to those in front. So we were all of one mind, not to take an inch backward while there was no actual restraint from taking one nearer home. We combined our efforts to encourage our guides, dwelt upon their inevitable suffering if they returned home to spend the winter, assured them that we would pay them promptly and see that they got comfortable quarters for the winter in Knoxville if they did not wish to go home with us. It was an anxious moment with us. If they abandoned us on that mountain, what would become of us? Not one of us knew anything about the mountain courses more than their general direction—not one of us could distinguish the ridges from the spurs—not one of us could tell north from south in that wild region after the sun went down; but with all this before us we could not think of going back forty or fifty miles to live three or four months with that gang of robbers. We not only offered to increase their compensation to any sum they might fix, but we begged, beseeched them not to turn back; but hearts full of fear, or minds full of mistrust, hears nothing and grants nothing, and as distressing as it was to us we parted—they to go home, we, we knew not whither.

CHAPTER VII.

SOUTH HOMINY CREEK, BUNCOMBE COUNTY, NORTH CAROLINA.
—UNCLE JIMMY SMITH—THAT DAY'S FIGHT BETWEEN THE
UNIONISTS AND REBELS—GEORGE PEOPLES—KIM DAVIS—
OUR NEXT GUIDE—A WEEK IN BUNCOMBE COUNTY—THE
GIRLS OF BUNCOMBE—FAREWELLS IN THE DAVIS FAMILY—
AGAIN IN THE MOUNTAINS—SANDY MUSH—ROCKY RIDGE—
MR. DUNN'S—THE MULES—FEDERAL PICKETS—KNOXVILLE—
THE OLD FLAG—HOW WE FELT—HOW WE LOOKED—GAY
STREET—GENERAL CARTER—IN A FEDERAL HOSPITAL—HOOD
BESIEGING NASHVILLE—ORGANIZATION FOR HOME VIA CUM-
BERLAND GAP—KIM HOME AGAIN—CONCLUSION.

Off to the right, six or seven miles, we could see a narrow strip of cultivated land following the meanderings of some stream, and here and there a column of smoke rising from a house.

Feeling the necessity for a guide to be absolute, and hoping to find one in the settlement to the right, as the only alternative we started down the side of the Pisgah in a hurry, for the shades of night already began to gather in the valley. The settlement we found bore the name of South Hominy Creek, Buncombe county, North Carolina. It was nearly dark when we got down the mountain. In the very point of the valley, where it was not more than a hundred yards wide, and where South Hominy Creek is nothing more than a gurgling rivulet, sat an unpretentious cabin, quiet as a tomb, and but for form of a man engaged near the door we should have pronounced it unoccupied. Crawling up within fifty yards of the cabin to make observations, we were soon all satisfied that the stooped and stiffened form before us was that of an old man; and Baker having on a full suit of rebel uniform, was soon over to see him.

We hoped to obtain the gentlemen's political principles in disguise. Baker being in rebel uniform, he could approach him directly upon that point; if a rebel, Baker could excuse himself and retire; if a Union man, he could call the rest of us to aid in convincing him that we were also. Baker summarily accosted Uncle Jimmy Smith, a diminutive, but as honored an old gentleman in his country as one of the same name is in ours, with:

"Grandpa, are you a rebel or a Union man?"

"What, sir?" replied Uncle Jimmy, straightening himself up.

"I want to know, just for fun, whether you are a rebel or a Union man?"

"What do you want to know that for?"

"Oh, I have heard you called both, and as I was passing, I just thought I would ask you."

"Well, sir, if it will do you any good to know, I will tell you that I was born under the old government, have lived eighty-two years under it, and I am an old man now, and want no better to die under. If this is not enough, I will add further, if you are a rebel soldier you will relieve me by passing on."

When we went rather hastily up upon Baker's whistle and motion, old Jimmy was much agitated, for he thought he had brought down some punishment upon himself by his acknowledgment. And now we had a tough time of it. We believed that he was a Union man, and knew ourselves to be, but the trouble was in persuading him to the same opinion. But the facts he detailed made it not seem strange to us that he should seem scrupulous. There had been that very day two companies of rebels, and one of them Indians, in the settlement, "after the boys," as he called them; by whom he meant the Union boys who had been pressed into the rebel army, and who had deserted and come home.

The facts in the case were these: They had been betrayed by just such strangers as we were. Ten days before two strange men, representing themselves as brothers named Muse, came to "the boys" on South Hominy Creek and implored protection—said they lived over in Transylvania county, and having deserted the rebel army to keep from fighting against the Union, it was impossible for them to remain about home and escape arrest; that knowing the facilities for hiding among the rugged peaks in Buncombe, they had come to beg a home with them for a few months, hoping to be able to compensate the friends for their board after the war was over. The credulous and hospitable boys committing the blunder of many such men—that of believing because they are honest, everybody else is so—received the Muses into their confidence without a suspicion.

It was Sunday evening that we went into the settlement, and on the evening before the Muse boys were unaccounted for, though no serious apprehensions were felt on account of the probability of their being among some of the friends in the neighborhood. Thoughtless of the dangers that were gathering, they drew their blankets about them in their mountain beds, to be awakened at dawn next morning by the militia, Indians and all, sweeping like an avalanche down the mountain upon them, led by the perfidious spies.

Up and at it, for liberty and life, from rock to tree and tree to rock they fought through all that Sunday, wounding and being wounded, two or three of them in their turn. Two were led away captives, but for the pleasure of locking the hand-cuffs upon two loyal men, the militia had the displeasure of binding up the wounds of as many more rebels.

Consequently, from this unexpected raid, the whole settlement was intensely excited; then is it surprising that old Jimmy Smith should sincerely believe that we were but a part of that rebel gang, and that we were feigning to be Yankees for some such purpose as the Muses had so successful wrought. So he did believe, at all events; and the earnestness with which he expressed his determination not to be betrayed, as the boys had been, was quite embarrassing to us. It vexes one always to be disbelieved when he tells the truth. It vexed us doubly here, for we told the whole truth about a matter in which it was so important that we should be believed. Old Jimmy urged us to go along and let him alone; he was too old to be mistreated, as well as too sharp to be caught on chaff. A happy thought came into Baker's head when he remembered that he had his commission in the 6th Missouri Federal Infantry in his pocket.

"Can you read writing, grandpa?"

"Yes."

"Well, here is my commission as First Lieutenant in the Yankee Army; examine it, if you please."

The reading of that paper alone, by the dim fire light in the house, convinced the old gentleman that we were really Federal soldiers. Then he lost not a moment in hurrying us off to hide, lest the rebels should be still in the neighborhood and drop in upon us any moment.

Old Jimmy was poor, very poor; living with his daughter while her husband was away in the rebel army; yet he was rich enough to have a good warm supper spread out before us in the bushes before eight o'clock.

Henry K. Davis was one of "the boys," rather the leader or commander among them; anyhow, so far as directing movements against the common enemy were concerned. He was represented to be a young man of high sense of honor, as well in his engagements as in his social relations, and to our encouragement had been twice through the mountains to Knoxville, and was at the time very desirous of leaving the South altogether for the North, if he could get some company.

To see Kim (for that was the name he bore among his neighbors) was now our heart's desire. I believe we had the impudence to ask Uncle Jimmy to conduct us three miles yet that night to the neighborhood of George Peoples, where it was expected we might find him. But the old man could not accommodate us; his eyes failed him after night, in his old age; then he had run about so much through the neighborhood during that day of excitement, that he was nearly exhausted. However, he promised to be off with us next morning by daylight, if we would stay where we were.

We made no attempt at sleep that night—did not even spread our blankets. The desertion of our guides, the effect of that day's raid in the settlement upon our prospects, the adventure expected to-morrow with Kim Davis and his men, were all subjects to be discussed.

With the much delayed dawn came Uncle Jimmy, tottering up the mountain with a basket on his arm, and a gun on his shoulder.

"What's the old man want with that gun?" anxiously inquired Good.

"I can't imagine," said Baker.

"I think I know," said Chisman, "he looks to me just like a Knownothing executioner, hunting for Irishmen; take heart, my boy, I'll plant a sprig of Cashew at your head, and write to your mother."

Uncle Jimmy explained it in another way. "You see," said he, "the rebels were all over the settlement yesterday, some of them may be lurking about here yet—my old gun can do us no harm, and if we should happen to get captured, I thought, by having my gun, I might shield myself and make your case no worse, by telling the rebels I had captured you, and was taking you to them—

then, as I return through the mountains, I might get a chance at a turkey, or a deer, or some other game."

George Peoples was a Mason, and Chisman thought he might use the "mystic chord" to our advantage; also, Mr. Peoples was a man of good information and eminently loyal. For these reasons it was thought prudent that we be conducted to his heighborhood, and placed under his direction, till a conference could be had with Davis.

We ate a hasty breakfast from the basket, and set out. Uncle Jimmy's activity surprised us; truly, too, it came near surpassing all of us. Though he tottered like an old tree, loose at the roots, he had a wonderful facility for getting over space. I do not think he walked a step the whole distance; it was run all the way. With his body bent forward at an angle of forty-five degrees, he went as rapidly through the mountains as a trained youth, stopping now and then to look or listen, with up-turned ear.

George Peoples was not at home; he had gone with two daughters on a week's journey into Transylvania county, to drive home some hogs. But his inestimable lady was there, who, directing uncle Jimmy to conduct us to a certain gorge, said that she would see that we lacked for nothing until Kim Davis could be found. The old gentleman led us up into the rocky gorge, and into a cluster of laurel bushes, and exhorting us to keep on the alert during the day, set out to hunt Davis, with the promise to report success that night, if possible.

About noon, two little girls came up with our dinner. In the evening the same two came again to tell us that their mother would expect us to take supper at the house, a little after dark; that their brother Wash., one of Davis' gang, would be there to see us.

At dark we went down, doubting nothing. Wash. met us on the barnyard fence, and astonished us by saying that he had been hiding all day in the same mountain, but a few hundred yards above us; that he had seen us several times moving about in the bushes, and two or three times had picked up his musket to shoot one, thinking that we were some skulking militia.

Mrs. P. soon announced her supper, and after the ordinary salutations, requested us to make haste to eat it and get back to the mountains, for she was always in mortal terror when any of the boys were about the house. The little girls were posted on each side of the house to watch; then we went to our seats at the table. Mrs. P. had many questions to ask; so had Wash., and the conversation was running glibly and merrily along, when suddenly two little girls came dashing into the house, stammering in a frenzied manner: "The militia are coming through the garden!"

Up to that moment we claimed to be equal to anybody in agility, but ever after that event we had a modified opinion of ourselves in that respect.

Wash., was sitting on a bench, next to the wall, hemmed in at both ends, when the alarm was given. On top of the bench, over the table, and out of the house he sprang, the back way, quicker than we could drop our pumpkin pie to follow him. We rushed in panic out the same way, only to get a glimpse of him as he flew across the barnyard toward the mountain. Wishing not to lose him, if we were to be pursued by the rebels, and hoping to gain something on a straight run, we threw down whatever encumbered us, and put into action our very best effort, but only to see ourselves more outdone than at the first. Before we got half across the barn yard, he was over the fence on the other side, flying up the mountain like the shadow to a hurrying cloud.

The occasion for running, however, was misconceived, and our clumsy locomotion was not particularly to our disadvantage. We four had but entered the woods, when Mrs. P., from the house, gently called Wash.; there being no answer, she called again, much louder than before—this time Wash. answered away up the mountain, three or four hundred yards ahead of us.

"Come back, Wash.; it's all right."

Wash. soon joined us again at the foot of the mountain, and the first thing he did was to excuse himself for his rather informal manner of leaving us; said he had been chased so much by the rascals, and had made such narrow escapes, that when they got after him now he had but little command of his judgment.

We all went back to the house to learn the cause of our alarm. As we approached the fence dividing the house from the barn yard, we discovered three men sitting there, with their guns lying on their laps in a careless way; we stopped—"Come one," says some one of the three; and Wash., being satisfied, led the way up to them.

It was Kim. Davis on the right, Wash. Curtis in the middle, and Mitch. Warren on the left, sent to us by the ever faithful uncle Jimmy. There was no introductions—not even a general mention of names. Kim. was satisfied that we were the men he had come to see, and we had a suspicion that he was the man we wanted to see.

Jumping off the fence, Kim. said, "Let's go up into the mountain and have a talk—this place is too much exposed."

He led the way to the identical gorge we had spent the day in, and seating ourselves together, he and his comrades proceeded to catechise us, perhaps as severely as the Vances, but in a manner vastly more civil. Civil, because they were not abusive, and because their procedure was eminently cunning and sagacious. It is hard to believe that men could have told a falsehood and escaped discovery. They would take us on all sides and by crossfire, at the same time, asking each of us a different question at the same time, pertaining to the same subject, and in no instance put a question in such a way that it would itself suggest the answer.

The examination having elicited nothing against us, Kim. became free to talk upon the subject desired. His remarks were, in substance, as follows:

"Yes, sir, I have made up my mind that I should like to go North, if I had any assurance of getting through the Northern army into the country, where I could throw away my gun. I am tired of this war—this man killing out of the army, as well as in the army—I've endured all that I'm willing to endure; have done enough to excuse me from more—like a slave to the field I was driven to the rebel army—marched six months in that treasonable array—since then I have lived two years in the mountains, watching for and hiding from an assassin all the time, and I'm now tired of the business. I have but little at stake in the contest anyhow—have no negroes to save, nor much property to protect, and I am so tired of hunting men's lives and hiding to save my own—I don't want to go into either army at this date. Your offer is liberal, but I want it understood that my services are not merchandise, to be bought and sold; and if I go with you it will be as a companion, and not as a servant. This is the only condition I will act upon: that you guarantee to me that when I have conducted you to Knoxville, you will conduct me north of the Ohio River, and protect me from the army."

The bargain was soon struck, but it grieved us to hear Mr. Davis say that he could not be ready to start before the following Sunday. However, we were not disposed to complain, for this time we felt confident that we were having to do with an honest and honorable man, who would act by us as he agreed, and in the meantime not fail to recognise us to be men worthy of some respect at least.

It was soon arranged among the companions that we should be conducted back to the neighborhood of uncle Jimmy and Evaline his daughter, to remain during the week of preparation, as it was regarded the most private and best place to hide of any in the settlement.

That night, however, we slept in the wood near Kim's father, and next morning before daylight went to the house for our breakfast. Asbury and Margaret A. Davis, Kim's parents, were getting old, and both very much concerned about the safety of their son—would have been much pleased with our arrangement with Kim. if they could have dismissed from their minds a suspicion that we might be spies, seeking to lead their boy to capture. But, amid the many dangers that surrounded him at home, with all their doubts and fears, I never heard that either of them opposed his embarking upon the trip. Next morning we went back to uncle Jimmy's, and were placed in his care for the week, the necessary provision being furnished by Kim. and his friends. Kim. then took his leave but first exhorting us to be of good cheer, for he would be ready promptly.

As it was in Henderson county, so it was in Buncomb with regard to the number of ladies that visited us while at uncle Jimmy's; nor did they come with empty hands or empty pockets. There is Rachel and Polly, and Matilda and Minerva, and Lucy and Sarah, whose fair forms even yet flit before me with hands full of chestnuts, choice apples, or other luxuries for us. Scarcely an hour passed in the day that some good thing was not laid at our feet from the hands of some loyal girl; and when they washed and mended up our miserable old rags till they were comfortable, we would have called them the kindest women in the world, if it had not been for the sisters in Henderson county. As it was, they were as kind as it was possible to be.

Notwithstanding we were among friends, and had plenty to eat, it seemed a long time till next Sunday morning. It was home that had our hearts many hundred miles away, over the wild, rugged, trackless mountains. No flowers, no birds, no fair women, no boon companions, no ambition could dissolve our fostered yearnings to be with friends at home, where we could lie down in peace, and speak of these times as by-gones.

Kim. was back from Haywood county, where he had gone to fix up some business long before his time, and was punctually at uncle Jimmy's Saturday evening to lead us to his father's. Sunday morning, the fourth day of December, 1864, we shook the frost from our blankets before three o'clock, and went to the house to arrange the preliminaries for starting. There was much trouble on this occasion in the Davis family. Asbury and Margaret, were both fond parents. They had spent many sleepless nights, and shed many tears when they knew their son was shivering in the mountain or being chased by some blood thirsty rebels; and because the authorities at Ashville had offered one thousand dollars reward for his arrest, it made the fond parents dote on him all the more. They had watched him and hid him for two years with dreadful solicitude, and now he was about to go from under their roof, perhaps forever, to a strange land, with strangers whom they nor he had ever seen or heard of a week before. Then thought they, these strangers may be spies decoying Kim. out to murder him, or they may all be captured on the way, or may be they will draft him into the Union army, and he get killed in battle, or may be they will cast him off, without money or friends, as soon as they get to the North. Such forebodings of evil crowded into the minds of these fond parents to culminate their trouble, particularly into that of the mother, who went about the house with streaming eyes to fix us off with every thing necessary for the trip.

This good woman and patriotic citizen has since been "gathered to her fathers" to be white-robed for her many virtues, and for the cross she bore during the war; but her spirit is still "hovering around" the persecuted loyal boys of South Hominy creek, who ate so often from her bounty and had so much of her sympathy, encouraging them to remain steadfast in their attachment to that government which was instituted and which is sought to be maintained in the interests of *all* men equally.

At seven o'clock in the morning the last words were spoken, and we were going across the field loaded like five pack mules, with sweet cakes and boiled ham.

Mitch. Warren and Wash. Curtis, loath to part with their companion, went with us a couple of miles into the mountains. The course we aimed to take because of its greater safety, would make the distance to Knoxville one hundred and sixty miles, over the roughest and wildest mountains in the range, hence we could hope to travel only by daylight. Kim. had been raised among the mountains: had chased deer and bears over them so much that he was not only active, but never made a mistake in direction. Our traveling now was very different from what it was with our former guides; we went right along now without a discord or a jealousy—driving ahead all the time in daylight, and sleeping together as boon companions after dark.

It would be hardly possible for men to work harder than we did during the seven days occupied by that trip. Our strength was employed to its utmost capacity every day. It was up and down, up and down the mountains all the time; stretching ourselves out to Vermonters as we pulled up one side, and staving ourselves up to Chinesemen going down the other side. And oh, dear, there is Sandy Mush; it makes my heart ache yet to think of that horrible mountain. Running backwards across a public highway to show our tracks in the other direction, then about face and up the almost perpendicular side of Sandy for a mile, all the time as much exposed to the gaze of any passer by as if we had been climbing a flag pole on a public square. Every muscle was called into action, and for the first hundred jumps I was in the van. But poor me, I failed, not for want of resolution, but strength. It was so steep that it really made my head swim to look back. I never would have got up, if it had not been for the huckleberry bushes, and the fear of rebel eyes. As it was, before the rest of us was half way, Kim. was lying on top shooting pebbles over our heads into the road a mile below; he ran up like a squirrel.

There, too, is Rocky Ridge, to which I do not "look backward with a smile." It was the only dangerous mountain we passed, and we had to pass it to keep our course. The peak of the Rocky Ridge, though rising but a little higher than its neighbors, stood like a mighty wall one hundred and fifty feet from top to base, with sides nearly perpendicular, and top or terrace for eight hundred yards, from four to ten feet wide; a single step to the right or left in a few places would have dashed us to pieces on the rocks below. We passed the place, too by moonlight, the first man getting on top from the shoulder of his comrade, then pulling the rest up, and sliding down at the other end on a pole.

On the night of the ninth of December we slept in a house, the first for seven months, within seven miles of Knoxville. It was in the house of a Mr. Dunn, an officer in our army, and whose house was a kind of general rendezvous for the Union men of that country. There were a half dozen such there that night, mostly traders to and from Knoxville. Next morning upon turning our faces towards the mountains that we had left but thirty-six hours before, we could but feel grateful to Him who regardeth even the sparrows, for they had cast about them a heavy mantle of snow, and their avenues closed for the winter. A fortunate escape.

One gentleman who staid all night at Mr. Dunn's was on his way to Knoxville to market with a couple of mules. Chisman, always on the alert for number one, saw the gentleman during the night with reference to a ride to the city, and in his arrangements did not forget his companion of ninety-nine troubles. Immediately after breakfast we strode one a piece of the divinely honored family, without saddle or bridle, but excellent rope halters, and trotted briskly off. We looked once back to our comrades trudging through the mud on foot, and wished they too had mules, but wished more to be ourselves in Knoxville. The master of the mules, a good humored sort of a man, let us have things pretty much our own way, and we spared neither rein nor switch till the towers of staunch old Knoxville loomed up in the distance: now we gave up our mules and sat down by the roadside to wait for our party. They soon came up, a little mad because we had ridden over five muddy miles without exchanging with them. Good, wiping the perspiration from his classic brow, remarked, "well, it's a bastely mane trick anyhow, that ye will ride five miles without letting us ride an inch." "Look out, goosey," replied Chisman, "remember that we have the Holstein to cross yet, and you know your weakness."

On the next range of hills nearer the city, we came upon a party of men sitting around a fire. They, failing to challenge us, Good shouted, "who sits there?" "Eighth Michigan Cavalry" was the reply. "Then give me a chew of Yankee tobacco, if you please." These were the Federal pickets. We only tarried long enough to answer a few general questions about our escape, and ask a few concerning the military situation. We were sadly disappointed to hear that Hood was besieging Nashville, and had destroyed all railroad communication with the North. But our cup of happiness still seemed full enough, to find once more Yankee bayonets at our backs, and Yankee friends in our front. We talked as glibly as we walked on, splashing through the mud. In the midst of our glee and air castles, we reached the top of a hill a half mile from town, and there, spread out before us in a grand panorama, was the city of Knoxville with her fortifications. To the left was the loved old flag, floating gloriously from the parapet of Fort Johnson. There was the Holstein, with her steamers smoking at the wharves. There was the long bridge stretching across her turbid waters. There was the park of army wagons. There was the tented field. There were Federal soldiers drilling on the lawn. There was the hum of industry wafted on the breeze—we stood a moment in silence; we looked congratulations at each other. We did not fall down and give up the ghost. We did not go into ecstacies. We did not hug each other as some have done. We did not cry. We simply felt good and went on.

As we approached the river a well dressed man came dashing up to us upon a horse with the air of a lord. He was a steamboat captain and accosted us with—

"Boys, do you want work?"

"Well, sir," retorted Chisman, "I don't know; what kind can you give us?"

"I want to hire four or five good strong hands for a few days to heave coal on my boat."

"Really," returned Chisman, "we would like exceedingly to accommodate you, but being United States army officers, the government will probably have work for us to do soon."

We crossed the river bridge and stood at the foot of Gay street parleying. We felt that our wardrobes were not in a suitable condition to appear in the streets of a fashionable city; yet it was necessary to reach the headquarters of the Provost Marshal General.

Chisman stood upon the uppers of a pair of Southern army brogans, bound to his feet with bark, and in the *frame* of a pair of Yankee pants, which but for the patches of red flannel and North Carolina linsey, would hardly have deserved the name, and which modestly or immodestly retired half way to the knees, leaving a touch of the Black Crook for exhibition. His sack coat was rather good and his cap tolerable, but such hair and beard were never seen on an honest man with opportunities. Our eccentric Irishman was the poorest one of all. Poor fellow, he left his last leather in the mountains, and on our way through Sevier county, Tennessee, begged the legs of a pair of brown jeans pants which he swaddled around his feet. The mud that he thereby carried, and the tracks that he made, were no fault of his but of the rags. He had been a prisoner twenty-two months, and had changed pants but once in the time. Those he had on had formerly been rebel, but like Chisman's was now in a state of dilapidation, and that for which I never did forgive him, one day as we lay in the woods, the rascal took my Columbia towel, and without my advice or consent made an important addition to one of the legs. His jacket was also rebel, but notwithstanding it was too short and a little out of fix at the elbows, when buttoned up, if he could have had on a shirt, his naked body would not have been seen. His hat I have lost sight of, but it was in keeping with the rest. As for Baker, he was the best dressed one of the party, having had a coat given him in North Carolina, and been an *adroit financier* in prison. The writer was next best. He had the worst hat of any, having no crown at all, but excepting his head and his feet he was comfortable but not gaudily attired. Kim. so recently from the supervision of his mother, was well enough to do.

Sunday seemed to be our transition day all along the journey—no important change in our affairs occurred on any other day. It was Sunday that we found the Union girls on the mountain in Henderson county; it was Sunday that the Vances deserted us on Pisgah, and when we found Uncle Jimmy Smith; it was Sunday that Kim Davis started with us from Buncombe county; and it was on Sunday that we stood in Gay street, in Knoxville, ready to report to Gen. Carter. It was just church going time, too, and the bells ringing out from every steeple in the city when we got our courage to the sticking point of making our way through the street to the headquarters of the General, unseemly as we were.

Good scraped the mud off his rags with a splinter the best he could; Chisman pulled down his pants; I pinned in the crown of my hat; and with Baker, the most genteel of any, in the lead, we took our accustomed Indian file up the sidewalk. Not one of us expected to blush or feel "harrowed up" by the citizens; for what should we care? We had come to our present state honorably, then probably there was not a single soul in the city to know us. But our *debut* was not eminently agreeable on account of the soldiers. They, as a rule, never were scrupulously severe in their practice of politeness. On this occasion they lampooned us at every street crossing. One chap, whose stature was fashioned very much like I have seen many Indianians, with six inches of Bologna in one hand and a loaf of bread in the other, squalled out to a party of marble players on the corner:

"Great Heavens, boys, look at these refugees coming in to draw our rations."

"Halloo, stranger, what will you take for your shoes? Say, Johnny, if you don't put weights to your pants, they will crawl over your head."

There were no replies, for we all knew too well the end of a soldier's tongue, to begin a retort with such a company.

Soon we stood at the door of General Carter's headquarters.

"Sentinel, be so kind as to say to the General that there are four officers who wish to see him at the door."

"Where are they?" mischievously inquired the boy.

"We are they, sir."

"Ha, ha, ha! you can't fool an old soldier. Orderly," says he to another youngster, writing a letter on a box, "go and tell the General that there are some refugees wanting to see him down here."

"No, sir," exclaimed Chisman, boiling over completely with wrath, "tell him that four United States officers, just escaped from prison at Columbia, are wanting to see him at the door. Any more impertinence out of you, sir," turning to the sentinel, "and I'll put you in the guardhouse, you young reprobate."

Gen. Carter received us very kindly, indeed. After hearing and noting down our full report of the condition of the South, he gave us an order upon the Quartermaster for whatever articles of clothing we might want that he had; then an order to be received into the Officers' Hospital, to depart at our pleasure.

Sure enough, Hood had destroyed the railroad below Nashville, and was at this time with his army, in their works around the city. Thus the only communication North was over-land, via Cumberland Gap, and the only way to reach home that winter, it then seemed, was to make another march of 190 miles through the Gap, to the railroad at Nicholasville Kentucky. But it consoled us some to learn that the wires were still working through the Gap, and that we could hear from home if we could not get there.

At the Quartermasters' we took a soldier's suit complete, from trooper's boots to high-topped hat, and with the things under our arms, we reported to the Surgeon in charge of Officers' Hospital. First we were shown to the bath room, where we were soon joined by four stout negroes, with soap, towels and flesh brushes, and after an hour of alternate perspiration and refrigeration, we came out of there in our new clean clothes, feeling very much improved by the exercise. Our next point was the barber shop, where the tonsorial art was applied to our faces and heads, and then to the telegraph office; and I lived longer and lived happier than I ever did before or since in the same length of time as the following went over the wires:

KNOXVILLE, Dec. 10th, 1864.

"E. H.—ESCAPED—WELL—WILL TRY TO BE HOME FOR CHRISTMAS. *_*

We spent the next four days in organizing and arming a party of sixty discharged soldiers and citizens for the trip to Nicholasville.

Early on the morning of the 14th, with muskets, twenty rounds of shot and ten day's rations, we selected from a lot of condemned horses such animals as we thought would carry us along briskly, but the roads were so bad, and our animals so weak, that, though we put forth our best effort, only succeeded in reaching Cincinnati Saturday night of Chrismas eve.

* * * * * * * * * *

Nine month's have now elapsed. In the meantime the war has collapsed and the armies dissolved.

Kim. Davis has spent his time at my brothers', and now, in September, 1865, goes back to see his friends in Buncombe. One day, in November, he and his father rode together to Ashville, and on their return they met one of the Muse boys, who had so wickedly betrayed him and his comrades the Sunday we arrived in their settlement. Muse, recognizing Kim., shouted out:

"Halloo, Davis; the war has settled all things even now hasn't it—how are you sir?" extending his hand.

Kim, failing to see the final adjustment, instead of accepting the proffered hand, drew his revolver and commenced firing at the rascal, but he escaped by jumping off his horse, over the fence, and running up a mountain.

A week afterwards, Kim. was arrested upon the charge of assault and battery, with intent to kill. He was tried upon the charge and sentenced to three months imprisonment in the jail, but the Governor, learning the provocation, remitted the punishment before it was all inflicted.

Thus it is told; and I would not wish to repeat it. This tedious sketch would never have been imposed upon the public by my own volition, had I not felt a desire to acknowledge, publicly, my appreciation of the services of the generous but humble individuals who gave it foundation. I mean the loyal Whites of North Carolina, and the Blacks of South Carolina. For whatever of liberty we obtained, perhaps whatever of life and health we now enjoy, whatever of delight we may feel in the narration of these events, whatever of merit may be awarded for this accomplishment, should all be ascribed to the unrequited kindness of these friends. Without their aid we would have been as powerless as the blind man. But the blacks, taking us by the hands on the banks of the Saluda, led us safely through the treacherous and treasonable State of South Carolina, to the mountains of North Carolina. There handing us over to the care of the loyal

Whites,, they led us triumphantly over the rough wilds, to our friends in Knoxville.

Therefore if this very unpretentious and imperfect narrative shall, even in the slightest degree, succeed in increasing the sympathy and action of the North in behalf of the loyal people of the South, who remained true and steadfast in all the trials of the war, then the labor and trouble it has cost, will be liberally compensated.

www.ingramcontent.com/pod-product-compliance
Lightning Source LLC
Chambersburg PA
CBHW031439160426
43195CB00010BB/781